non multum in Parvo
Sed Parvum in Multo.

10888
H

GUIDE,
&c.

Directions to Strangers,

Shewing the Chief Things of

CURIOSITY and NOVELTY

In the City and Suburbs

WITH

Short Descriptions of the Courts, PALACES,
Churches, Charity, Gardens, Squares,
and all the ancient and noble Structures in
and near this famous Metropolis. Also of Oxford, Cambridge, Windsor, Hampton-Court, Blackheath,
Chelsea, Kensington, and Greenwich.

To which is added,

The Rates of Hackney-Coaches and Boats.

... in Latin and English. For the Use of
Foreigners and Strangers.

The Second Edition, Corrected and Enlarged.

LONDON:

NEW

Guide to London:

OR,

Directions to Strangers;

Shewing the Chief Things of

CURIOSITY and NOTE

In the City and Suburbs.

WITH

Short Descriptions of the COURTS, PALACES, CHURCHES, CHAPELS, COLLEGES, SQUARES, and all the ancient and noble STRUCTURES in and near this famous Metropolis. Also of Oxford, Cambridge, Windsor, Hampton-Court, Richmond, Chelsea, Kensington, and Greenwich.

To which is added,

The Rates of HACKNEY-COACHES and BOATS.

In *French* and *English*. For the Use of Foreigners and Strangers.

The Second Edition, Corrected and Enlarged.

LONDON:

Printed for J. SMITH near *Exeter-Change* in the *Strand*, T. BOWLES in St. *Paul's* Church-yard, J. BOWLES over-against *Stocks-Market*, and at *Mercers-Hall* in *Cheapside*. M,DCC,XXVI.

LE NOUVEAU

Guide de Londres:

OU,

Instructions pour les Étrangers;

Contenant ce qu'il y a de plus

CURIEUX & de plus REMARQUABLE

Dans la Ville & les Fauxbourgs.

AVEC

Une COURTE Description des PALAIS, tant Roïaux que Particuliers, des EGLISES, CHAPELLES, COLLEGES, PLACES, & de tous les anciens & nobles EDIFFICES de cette fameuse Metropole. Comme aussi des Universites d'Oxford, & de Cambridge, de Windsor, Hampton-Court, Richmond, Chelsea, Kensington, & Greenwich.

A quoi on ajoute

Les Prix des COCHES, & des BATEAUX.

En Françoise & en Anglois : Pour la Commmodité des Etrangers.

Seconde Edition, Corrigée & Augmentée.

A LONDRE.

Chez J. SMITH pres du Exeter-Change dans le Strand, T. BOWLES dans le Cemitere de St. Paul, J. BOWLES vis a vis Stocks-Market & au Mercers-Hall dans Cheapside. MDCCXXVI.

NOUVEAU

Guide de Londres

ou

Instructions pour les Étrangers

Contenant ce qu'il y a de plus

Curieux & de plus Remarquable

Dans la Ville & les Fauxbourgs.

AVEC

Les Colleges, Défensés du Parc, les Paroisses, les Églises, Chapelles, College de Black... Gresham, les Marchés, & les Écoles de ces Écoles à Oxford, & à Cambridge, Hampton-Court, Stenmouth, Chelsea, & Greenwich.

Les Prix des Coches, & des ...

La Maniere de ...

TO THE

Reader.

THE former Editions of this Book being entirely sold off, the Author was desir'd to correct, amend and enlarge this *Guide of London,* which is so necessary to all who come to this great Metropolis, and particularly to Foreigners, whose chief Design being only to see the chief Curiosities of Countries, Cities and Places, find themselves at a great loss when there is not some short Relation thereof printed,

AU

Lecteur.

LES premieres Editions de ce Livre etant entierement *Vendues,* l'Autheur a eté prié de corriger & augmenter ce Guide de Londres, *si necessaire* a tous ceux qui viennent dans cette grande Capitale, & particulierement aux Etranger dont le principal But n'etant que de voir les Curiosités les plus remarquables des Pais, Villes & Lieux, se trouvent en peine de les decouvrir lors qu'il n'y a point de

A 3   *Rela-*

To the Reader.

ted, to hint, as it were, where those Antiquities and Curiosities are to be found. Tho' we have follow'd this Plan in this Edition, we can assure you it is much larger and more exact than the preceding: We have not thought fit to make the Curious follow the Tours which the Author of the former Editions prescribed to them, but rather leave it to every one to see such Places as his Inclination or Affairs will permit him: Therefore we begin at the Royal Palace of St. *James*'s, and direct you through the Park to *Whitehal*, the *Cockpit*, *Westminster-Abby*, the House of Lords, House of Commons, *Westminster-Hall*, and thence thro' the *Strand*, &c. to the *Tower* of *London*, giv-ing

Au Lecteur.

Relations imprimée qui leur indique où ils trouveront ces Antiquités & Curiosités. Quoique nous ayons suivi ce Plan dans cette Edition, nous pouvons vous assurer qu'elle est plus ample & plus exacte que les precedentes: Nous n'avons pas jugé a propos d'obliger les Curieux de suivre les Tours que l'Autheur des Editions precedentes leurs avoit prescrit aimant mieux que chacun voye les Lieux que son Inclination, ou ses Affaires lui permettra. C'est pourquoi nous commençons par le Palais de St. James, *& vous dirigeons par le Parc à* Whitehal, *au* Cockpit, *a l'Abbaye de* Westminster, *a la Chambre des Seigneurs, a celle des Communes, à* Westminster-Hall, *& de la par le* Strand, *à la* Tour *de* Lon-

To the Reader.

ing you as exact a Description of each Place you meet in your Way thither, as the brevity of this small Treatise, or rather the vast number of noted Places, ancient or noble Structures, can allow; and bring you back again thro' the *Minories, Moorfields, Smithfield, Holbourn, St. Giles's,* and all the new Buildings both near *Red-Lyon-Fields, Hanover-Square,* &c. to *St. James's,* describing the other Places, Suburbs, Hamlets, Districts, Towns, Palaces, Hospitals, Halls and Colleges, in and near this famous Metropolis, that the Curious may view them if they please. We add also a description of the Palaces of *Kensington, Richmond, Hampton-Court,*

Au Lecteur.

Londres, vous donnant une Description exacte de tous les Endroits que vous trouvez en Chemin, faisant autant que la brievité de ce petit Traité, ou plutot le grand nombre d'Endroits memorables, de Structures anciennes, ou superbes, le permettent, & vous en ramenons par les Minories, les Moorfields, Smithfield, Holbourn, *St.* Gilles, *& tous les nouveaux Batimens tant près de* Red-Lion-Fields, *que de* Hanover-Square, *à* St. James, *decrivant les autres Lieux, Faux-bourgs, Hameaux, Quartiers, Villes, Palais, Hopitaux, Halles, & Colleges dedans & aux environs de cette fameuse Capitale, afin que le Curieux les puissent examiner s'il leur plait. Nous ajoutons aussi*

Count, *Windsor*, of the Universities of *Oxford* and *Cambridge*, of the Castle of *Bleinheim*, and Royal Hospitals of *Greenwich* and *Chelsey*; and the Rates of Hackney-Coaches, Stage-Coaches, and Boats.	*aussi une description du Palais de Kensington, Richmond, Hampton-Court, Windsor, des Universitez d'Oxford & de Cambridge, du Château de Bleinheim, des Hopitaux de Chelsey & de Greenwich; & les Prix des Fiacres, Coches & Bateaux.*

The

The Guide of LONDON.

LONDON, the Metropolis of the *British* Monarchy, is the greatest, most, populous, and flourishing City in the Universe: It is situated at 51 Deg. 30 Min. of Latitude on the famous and beautiful River of *Thames*. And it is thought this Situation gave it its Name, which formerly was *Llondin*, which in the old *British* Language signified *Town of Ships*, or *Ship-Town*; from whence, by Corruption, it has been changed to *London*. Its Length from *Lime-house* to *Tuttle-Street* is about seven Miles and an half; and its Breadth from *Black-*

Le Guide de LONDRES.

LONDRES *Capitale de la Monarchie Britanique, est la plus grande, la plus Peuplée, & la plus Florissante Ville de l'Univers. Elle est situèe a 51 Deg. 30 Min. de Latitude. Sur la fameuse & belle Riviere de la Thamise, & on croit que cette situation lui a donné son Nom, qui ce devant étoit* Llondin, *ce qui en vieux* Bretton *signifioit Ville de Vaisseaux, & qui par Corruption a eté changé en* London. *Sa Longueur depuis* Lime-house *jusqu'à* Tuttle-street *est de pres de 2 Lieues & demie; & sa largeur depuis* Blackman-street *en* Southwark, *jusqu'a l*

B   *Eglise*

Blackman-street in South-wark to St. *Leonard's* Shoreditch, is very near three Miles. It contains above 5400 Streets, Lanes, and Allies, some of which are as Spacious and as fine as any in *Europe.*

When a Stranger is come to the Place he is directed to, we suppose his first desire is to see the Court, and therefore in order to shun the Throng which the Streets of *London* are always crowded with, he may take a Hackney-Coach and go through the *Pall-Mall*, which is a fine Street, in which, among other fine Buildings, is *Schomberg*-House, a Stately and fine Structure, And at the end of the said Street, on the Left-hand, you come to

St. James's Palace.

THis is the King's usual Place of Residence during the Winter; and you must not be surpriz'd if it does not an

---

Eglise de St. *Leonard* en Shorditch, est de près d'une Lieuë. Elle contient plus de 5400 Ruës ou Ruettes dont il y a des Ruës qui sont aussi belles & aussi larges qu'il y en ait en Europe.

Lors qu'un Etranger vient au Lieu où il est adressé nous supposons qu'il souhaite de commencer par voir la Cour, c'est pourquoi afin d'eviter la foule qu'il y a toujours dans les Ruës de Londres, il prenda un Fiacre & ira par le Pall-Mall qui est une belle Ruë ou entr'autres beaux Edifices il y a l'Hotel de Schomberg, qui est un Beau & superbe Batimens; & au bout de la dite Ruë a la Gauche vous venez au

Palais de St. James.

C'Est icy où le Roi fait l'Hyver sa Residence, & vous ne devez pas etre surpris s'il ne repond pas a l'Eclat que l'on devoit atten-

answer the Magnificence of a Royal Palace, and particularly the Palace of a King of *Great-Britain*. But this House was built by Cardinal *Wolsey*, for the use of Leprous Women: And after the Cardinal's Death they yielded it to King *Henry* VIII. for a Pension which he gave them for Life. It has since been enlarg'd, and some Princes or Princesses of the Blood have resided therein: Princess *Anne* of *Denmark* afterwards Queen *Anne*, lived there many Years, before and after she was Queen, because the Palace of *Whitehall* (where the Kings resided in the Winter) was burnt down in the Year 1698. and the burthensome Wars *England* has since been involv'd into, have hinder'd the building another Palace, or the rebuilding of *Whitehall*.

When you go into this Palace, by the Way abovesaid, you enter it through a Gate which brings you into a Court where a Company mounts

s'attendre de trouver à un Palais Royal, & sur tout au Palais d'un Roy d'Angleterre. Mais vous sçavez que cette Maison fut batie par le Cardinal Wolsey pour des Filles Lepreuses, qui après sa mort, le cederent a Henry VIII. pour une Pension Viagere qu'il leur donna. Depuis ce tems là on l'a agrandi, & les Princes ou Princesses du sang y ont quelques fois Residé; la Princesse Anne de Dannemarc qui fut depuis la feue Reine Anne, y a demeuré plusieurs Années, & meme durant son Regne, parce que le Palais de Whitehall (où les Rois faisoient leur sejour durant l'Hyver) avoit eté brulé dès l'An. 1698. & que les Guerres Onereuses que la Nation a eu depuis ce tems là, l'ont empechée d'en batir un autre, ou de rebatir Whitehall.

En entrant dans ce Palais par St. James's-street, vous passez par une Porte qui vous conduit dans une Cour où une Compagnie monte la Garde. Et au

mounts the Guard. And at the end of the Piazzas you come directly to the great Stairs that leads to the King's Apartments; at the upper-end of these Stairs you come into the Guard-Room of the Yeomen of the Guards, who, in this Country, have the same Rank and Duty as the *Swiss* Guards have abroad, their Dress being almost the same. There are Arms in this Room finely put up, and kept very neat. From thence you come into a fine State-Room where there is a rich Canopy, the King gives Audience to the Ambassadors in this Room. Thence you enter the Great Room on the Right-hand, at the end of which is the Great Drawing-Room, where every *Sunday, Monday, Wednesday,* and *Friday,* the Nobility, the Ministers, &c. meet, and where all Strangers, above the Inferior Rank, may see the King, the Prince and Princess, who come there regularly on the aforesaid Nights, as also

bout de l'arcade vous venez directement au grand l'Escalier qui vous conduit à l'Apartement du Roi; au haut de l'Escalier vous entrez dans la Sale des Halebardiers, qui en ce païs cy tiennent lieu de Gardes Suisses, & ont un Habit qui approche du leur. Il y a dans cette Sale des Armes tres propres, tres bien rangées. De là vous avancez dans une tres belle Sale ou il y a un Beau Dais, c'est dans cette Chambre que le Roi donne Audience aux Ambassadeurs. De là vous entrez dans la Grand Sale à Droite qui vous mène à la Grande Antichambre, ou se trouve tous les Dimanches, Lundy, Mecredy, & Vendredis la Noblesse, qui compose le Cercle, & ou tous les Etrangers peuvent aller voir le Roi, le Prince, & la Princesse, qui y viennent Regulierement tous les soirs Susdits; & les Jeunes Princesses y viennent tres souvent avec Madame la Comtesse de Portland leur Gouvernante. En sortant

also the young Princesses who frequently come there with the Countess of *Portland* their Governess. As you come out of these Rooms you go on forwards to the King's Closet Apartments, &c. which you may see if he is out of Town: They have a Communication to the Apartments that belonged to the Prince of *Wales* when he was at St. *James's*. This Palace has been considerably enlarg'd within a few Years towards the *West*, and some Apartments were added to it towards the *East* when the Prince liv'd there. The Gardens are pretty fine, and the Chapel, tho' plain, is very commodious. Strangers ought not to omit going thither some *Sunday*, to see the King pass to his Chapel, when he goes thither, being always preceded by a Peer of the Realm carrying a Sword of State before His Majesty, who is attended by the Lord of the Bedchamber in Waiting, and accompanied by their Royal

sortant de ces Chambres à Droite, vous trouvez les Apartemens le Cabinet, &c. du Roi, que vous pourrez voir s'il est hors de ville, & lesquels ont Communication aux Apartemens qui etoient au Prince de Galles, lors qu'il etoit à St. James. Cette Maison a été agrandie très Considerablement depuis quelques Années sur tout vers l'Occident, & on y a fait quelques Apartemens vers l'Orient, lorsque Monseigneur le Prince y demeuroit. Les Jardins en sont assez beaux, & la Chapelle quoi qu'assez Simple est très commode. Les Etrangers ne doivent pas manquer d'aller le Dimanche voir passer le Roi lors qu'il y va, etant toujours precedé d'un Pair du Royaume portant l'Epée d'Etat devant sa Majesté, qui est accompagné du Seigneur de sa Chambre qui est de quartier, & suivi de leurs Altesses Royales, des Ministres Etrangers, & de la Noblesse; les Gentilshommes de la Bande

Royal Highnesses, the Foreign Ministers, and the Nobility; the Gentlemen of the Band of Pentioners with their golden Pertuisans closing the March. There are several Courts and good Apartments in this Palace, and King *George* has built Stables and Coach-Houses there. Beside the Chapel-Royal there is another for the *Germans*, and another which Queen *Catharine*, Spouse to King *Charles* II. had built for the *Roman* Catholicks, and which has been, since the Revolution, given to the *French* and *Dutch* Protestants, who preach therein alternatively every *Sunday*. Going out of this Palace towards the *East*, you find

des Pensionaires ayant chacun leurs Hache ou Pertuisanne d'Or ferment la Marche. Il y a plusieurs Cours dans ce Palais, & le Roy George y a fait batir des Ecuries & des Remises. Outre la Chapelle Royale il y en a une pour les Allemands, & une autre, que la Reine Catherine, Epouse de] Charles Second, avoit fait batir pour les Catholiques Romains; mais qu'on a donne depuis la Revolution aux François & aux Hollandois Reformés, qui y prechent Alternativement. En sortant de ce Palais vers l'Orient, vous trouvez

Mark

Marlborough-House.

THe late Duke of that Name built it. It is very fine and magnificently Furnish'd; but what raises most its lustre are the Pictures of the Victories which that famous and invincible General gain'd; and which he has placed in this House, they well deserve the Notice of the Curious. From thence you go into the Park of St. *James's*, its Mall, Walks, &c. are very fine, and with its Canal make exactly the Figure of an Harp. At the End of the Mall towards the *West*, you have the beautiful

Buckingham-House.

ITs Situation sets off the Beauties of it; but one may say, it is a Jewel in its kind. Its Structure, Motto's, Statues, Fountain, Ornaments, in short, every thing thereto belonging dis-

L'Hotel de Marlbor

LE feu Duc de ce Nom l'a fait batir. Il est tres beau & magnifiquement Meublé; mais ce qui en releve le plus l'Eclat, sont les Tableaux des Victoires que ce fameux & invincible General a gagné, & qu'il y a fait representer, ils meritent bien l'attention des Curieux. De là vous entrez dans le Parc de St. James dont le Mail, les Allées, &c. sont tres beaux & qui avec son Canal font exactement la Figure d'une Harp. Au bout du Mail vers l' Occident vous trouvez le bel

Hoteld-Buckingham

SA Situation en releve la Beauté, mais on peut dire que c'est un Bijoux. Sa Structure, ses Devises, ses Statues, sa Fontaine, ses Ornemens, tout enfin y fait voir l' excellent Gout du feu Duc de Buck-

discover the exquisite Taste of the late Duke of *Buckingham* who built it. From thence you may walk round the Park and see the little Square call'd

Queen-Square.

IT is only a Court, in which the late Queen's Statue is placed, but it is very neat and the Houses in it are very fine. Thence going to the *East* you will come to a kind of Cupola, which is the Cock-Pit, where there were Cock-fightings formerly, it is a Diversion greatly admired by the *English* only: and as these Cocks fight so furiously that they often kill one another, considerable Wagers are laid on their Heads; but this Cock-Pit is no more frequented; and that behind *Grays-Inn* has the only vogue. We shall speak of it in its Place. Going on still towards the *East* you will come to the Horse-Guards, where the King's Horse-Guards, Horse-Gre-

Buckingham *qui la fait bâtir. De là vous pourrez faire le tour du Parc, & voir le petit quarré appellé*

Queen-Square.

CE *n'est qu'une Cour dans laquelle on a placé la Statue de la Reine* Anne, *mais elle est très propre & les Bâtimens en sont très beaux. Vous trouverez ensuite vers l'Orient une Espece de Dome qu'on appelle le* Cock-Pit, *c'est où les Coqs se battoient autrefois, c'est un Divertissement que le seuls* Anglois *aiment beaucoup, & comme ces Coqs se battent si furieusement qu'ils se tuent ordinairement, il s'y fait des Gageures Considerables. Mais on ne fréquente plus ce* Cock-Pit *ici, & on va à celui qui est derriere* Grays-Inn, *dont nous parlerons en son lieu. De là en suivant toujours vers l'Orient vous viendrez à la Grande Garde, où les Gardes*

Grenadiers and Foot-Guards daily do Duty. Under the Dial is a spacious Room, where there is Preaching of a *Sunday*, and the Board of General Officers and General Court-Martials are held on the other Week-Days: It is also the Office of the Judge Advocate General of the Army. And crossing the Street, over-against this Guard, you come to the

du Corps, *Grenadiers à Cheval*, & *Gardes à Pied* montent la Garde. Dessous le *Quadran* est une spacieuse Sale où l'on preche le *Dimanche* & où ce qu'on appelle le *Board des Officiers Generaux* ou pour mieux dire le *Grand Conseil de Guerre* & *la Cour des Officiers Generaux* se tient. C'est aussi le Bureau du Juge Avocat General de l'Armée. En traversant la Grande Rüe vous venez à l'Ancien

Palace of *Whitehal.*

Palais de *Whitehal.*

THis Palace, as large as it was, was not a Royal Palace, Cardinal *Wolsey* had built it for a Palace to the Archbishops of *York*; and as the ancient Royal Palace at *Westminster* was reduced to Ashes, this said Cardinal gave it to King *Henry* VIII. who made some Additions to it; when it was burnt, as we have said, in 1698, and nothing of it remains except the Banqueting-House. It was from one of the walled Windows of this House

CE *Palais* tout grand qu'il étoit n'étoit pas un *Palais Royale* le Cardinal Woolsey l'avoit fait batir pour être le *Palais des Archeveques d'York*; & comme l'ancien *Palais Royal de Westminster* fut reduit en Cendres; ce Cardinal le ceda au Roi Henry VIII. qui y fit faire quelques Additions, & ces Successeurs l'avoient beaucoup agrandi lorsqu'il fut brulé comme nous l'avons dit en 1698, & il n'en reste que le *Banqueting-House*; c'est à dire la *Maison des Banquets.*

House that the unfortunate King *Charles* the First went to the Scaffold, where his Head was cut off. You may see the Chapel which is at the first Story of this House, and which is very fine, the Ceiling having been Painted by the famous *Rubens*. It is now supplied by 24 Chaplains, drawn from both Universities, who send twelve each every Year, two of whom officiate alternatively a Month each, and receive 30 *l.* a piece for that Service from the King. This Noble Establishment was lately made by King *George*.

Above this Chapel there are fine Apartments where the foreign Ministers, when they make their Publick Entry are treated during three Days at the King's Charge, whence it is called the *Banqueting-House*. In the Privy-Garden and before this House there is a Pedestrian

quets. *Ce fut par une des Fenetres murées de cette Maison que l'Infortuné Roi Charles Premier passa pour descendre sur l'Echafaut, ou on lui trancha la Tête. Vous pourrez voir la Chapelle qui est au premier Etage de cette Maison & qui est tres belle, le Plat-fond en a été Peint par le fameux* Rubens. *Et elle est a present desservie par 24 Chapellains qui se tirent de l'une & de l'autre de deux Universités, qui par consequent en envoyent douze chacune tous les Ans, dont deux y officient alternativement un Mois durant & reçoivent 30 Livres Sterlin chacun du Roy pour ce service. C'est le Roy* George *qui vient de faire ce noble & necessaire Etablissement. Au dessus de cette Chapelle il y a de beaux Apartemens où l'on regale pendant trois Jours aux Depens du Roy, les Ambassadeurs & Ministres Etrangers apres leurs Entrée Publique; de la vient qu'on l'appelle la Salle des* Banquets. *Devant ce Batiment dans la Cour Interieure, on voit une Statue Pedestre de* Jaques

...trian Statue in Brass of King *James* II.; and above this House is the famous Weather-Cock which the said King put up there in order to see from his Windows whether the Wind was favourable for the Prince of *Orange*'s Fleet, when he was preparing to land in *England* in 1688. As all the Ground of this Palace has been given to several Lords, who have built Houses thereon, it is not like to be rebuilt. It is at *Whitehal* that the War and Army Debenture Offices are kept. As you come out of *Whitehal* you find on your Left a Gate of *Gothick* Order, which is very fine; there are some ancient Heads on it which were excellent, but are damag'd by Time. And going through that Gate, you come to a little Door that brings you to the *Cock-Pit*, where the Secretary of States Office, the Treasury, and the Council Chambers are, and where you find nothing Great nor Admirable, except those unwearied

Jaques II. en Bronze; & au dessus de la Maison est la Girouëtte que le dit Roy Jaques y fit mettre afin de pouvoir observer de ses fenetres, si le vent etoit favorable pour la Flotte du Prince d'Orange, lors qu'il se preparoit a venir faire descente en Angleterre en 1688. Comme tout le Terrain de ce Palais a eté donné à plusieurs Seigneurs qui s'y sont fait batir des Maisons il n'y a pas d' apparence qu'on le rebatisse. C'est a Whitehal qu'est le Bureau & l'Office du Secretaire des Guerres. En sortant de Whitehal vous trouvez a Gauche une Porte d'Ordre Gothique qui est tres belle on y voit quelques Tetes Antiques, qui ont été excellentes mais qui sont endommagées par le Tems. En passant cette Porte, vous venez a une petite Porte qui vous conduit au Cock-Pit, où sont les Bureaux des Secretaires d' Etats, de la Tresorerie, & la Chambre du Conseil & où on ne trouve rien de Grand ni de Remarquable, que ces Infatiguables &

habiles

wearied and skilful Ministers of State, who so worthily hold the Reins of Government, and whose consummate Wisdom, animated by that of their august and undaunted Sovereign, prescribe, and on many Occasions, give Rules and Laws to almost all the Universe. As soon as you are come through that little Door, you find on your Right-hand the Office of His Grace the Duke of *Newcastle*, Secretary of State. A little farther, on your Left, there is a very fine Tennis-Court; and at the end of the Alley there is the Office of the Treasury; and going up the Great Stairs you come to the Office of the Lord Viscount *Townshend* Secretary of State; and at the Second Story is that of the Secretary of State for *Scotland*, who is now the Duke of *Roxburgh*. These two have a View over the Park, as well as the Treasury. The Council-Chamber is near the Lord *Townshend's* Office.

From

babiles Ministres d'Etat qui tiennent si dignement les Renes de l'Etat, & dont la Sagesse consommée animée de celle de leur auguste, & intrepide Souverain prescrivent en tant d'Occasions des Regles, & donnent des Loix a presque tout l'Univers. Des que vous etes entré par cette petite Porte, vous trouvez a Droite le Bureau du Duc de Newcastle Secretaire d'Etat. Un peu plus haut a Gauche, il y a un tres beau Jeu de Paume ou Tripot; & au bout de l'Allée est le Bureau des Finances, ou la Tresorerie; & en montant le Grand Escalier qui s'y trouve, on vient au Bureau dus Secretaire d'Etat, qui est a present le Lord Vicomte de Townshend; & au second Apartement est celui du Secretaire d'Etat pour l'Ecosse qui est a present le Duc de Roxburgh. Ces deux derniers Bureaux & celui des Finances donnent sur le Parc. Le Chambre du Conseil est proche le Bureau de My Lord Townshend.

From hence you go by *King-street* to the

Abbey of Westminster.

THis Abbey is famous for its Antiquity, seeing it is certain that *Sibert* first *Saxon* King of *Eastsex* who was converted to the Christian Faith, was the Founder thereof, and dedicated it to St. *Peter*, in the Year 612. It is true, they attribute a much ancienter Origin to it, but it has no other Foundation than the Dreams of the Monks. It is in this Abbey that, by virtue of a Bull of Pope *Nicholas* all the Kings of *England* were to be crowned, and tho' the Reformation has abolish'd all the Power of the Papal Bulls in this Kingdom, yet the Kings are always crown'd, and commonly buried there. Besides several fine and noble Monuments and Tombs, there are the two Chairs wherein the Kings and Queens are crown'd,

under

En sortant d'ici, vous pourez vous faire conduire à

L'Abbaye de Westminster.

CEtte Abbaye est célèbre par son Antiquité puis qu'il est certain que Sibert premier Roi Saxon d'Essex, qui embrassa le Christianisme en fut le fondateur, & la dedia a St. Pierre environ l'An de Grace 612. Il est vray qu'il lui donne un Origine beaucoup plus Ancienne, mais elle n'a d'autre fondement que les Reveries des Moines. C'est dans cette Abbaye qu'en vertu d'une Bulle du Pape Nicholas on devoit couronner tous les Rois d'Angleterre, & quoique la Reformation ait aboli tout le pouvoir des Bulles Papales en ce Royaume, les Rois s'y font toujours Couronner & y sont ordinairement Enterrés. Outre plusieurs beaux Monumens & Tombeaux, on y voit les deux Chaises de Bois dans lesquelles on couronne les Rois & les Reines

Soin

Under the most ancient is a Stone which is pretended to be the same that the Patriarch *Jacob* lean'd his Head upon when he saw the Ladder on which the Angels came down from and went up to Heaven, and of which 'tis said by these two pretended Prophetical Verses, That the *Scots* should reign where-ever it should be transported.

Ni fallat fatum, Scoti quocumque Locatum
Inveniunt Lapidem, regnare tenentur ibidem.

Edward the First brought this Stone from *Scotland* in 1298, and it was but in 1603, that is, 305 Years afterwards that *James* the Sixth of *Scotland*, and first of the Name of *England*, came to the Crown of this Realm.

There are also the Remains of Queen *Catharine* Wife to *Henry* the Fifth, and Daughter to *Charles* the Sixth of *France* call'd the *Simple*: This Corps, which is yet Sound, had been till now intire had not

Sous la plus ancienne il y a une *Pierre*, qu'on pretend etre la meme qui servit d'oreiller au Patriarche *Jacob*, lors qu'il vit en songe l'*Echelle* sur laquelle les Anges montoient & descendient du Ciel, & dont on a dit par ces deux vers pretendus Prophetiques ; *Que les Ecossois regneroient en quelque Lieu que cette Pierre seroit transportée.*

Ni fallat fatum, Scoti quocumque Locatum
Inveniunt Lapidem, regnare tenentur ibidem.

Edward Premier l'apporta d'Ecosse en 1298, & ce ne fut qu'en l'An 1603 scavoir 305 Ans apres que *Jaques* Six d'Ecosse, & premier du Nom d'*Angleterre* parvint a la Couronne de ce Royaume.

On y voit aussi le Corps de la Reine *Catherine* Femme de *Henry* V. d'Angleterre & Fille de *Charles* VI. de France dit le *Simple* : Ce Corps qui est encore Sain seroit tout entier, si les Catholiques

not the *Roman* Catholicks (who believe her a Saint) cut off and carried away several Parts thereof. There is also the Sword King *Richard* used in the Wars against the *Saracens* in the Holy Land. You must not sit down in those Chairs, nor touch either of those Relicks, unless you will expose yourself to forfeit a Shilling or Six-Pence.

There are three Wax Effigies in this Abby, *viz.* that of King *Charles* II. that of General *Monk*, who restor'd that Monarch, and that of the charming late Dutchess of *Richmond*, who is in the same Cloaths and Ornaments she wore at the Coronation of K. *William* and Q. *Mary*. You will also observe the exquisite Workmanship of King *Henry* the Seventh's Chapel, at the top of the Cornish of which there are Figures in Freestone representing one in the Dress of all the Religious Orders of Monks, Nuns, &c. in the *Roman* Church. This Abby has since been lately

liques Romains qui la re-gardent comme une Sainte, n'en avoient coupé & emporté plusieurs morceaux. Il y a aussi l'Epée dont le Roy Richard s'est servi dans la Terre Sainte contre les Sarazins. Il ne faut ni s'asseoir dans ces Chaises, ni toucher à ces Reliques, &c. a moins qu'on ne veuille s'exposer à payer une Amende d'un Chellin ou de six Sous.

Il y a dans cette Abbaye trois Statues ou Effigies de cire scavoir celles du Roy Charles II. du General Monk, qui remit ce Monarque sur le Throne, & celle de la charmante Duchesse de Richemont qui est dans les Memes Habits & Ornemens qu'elle porta au Couronnement du Roy Guillaume & de la Reine Marie. Vous aurez aussi soin d'y remarquer le Travail exquis, de la Chapelle de Henry Sept au haut de la Corniche de laquelle il y a en pierre de Taille des Figures Habillées de la Maniere dont s'habillent tous les differens Ordres de Religieux & Religieuses de l'Eglise Romaine.

lately repaired You must pay Three-pence to see the Tombs, Six-pence to see the Corps of Queen *Catherine*, and a Trifle to him that shews them to you: The Church gets by every thing. There are round this Abby very fine Monuments, which you are not to omit to see and read their Inscriptions. The Place where Divine Service is performed is pretty singular, observe the Altar and the Hangings. Thence you must go to the

Romaine. On a depuis peu reparé cette Abbaye. On paye trois Sous pour voir les Tombeaux, six Sons pour voir le Corps de la Reine Catherine, & on donne une bagatelle à celui qui vous la fait voir. L'Eglise gagne à tout. Il y a eut autour de cette Abbaye de beaux Tombeaux, que vous ne manquerez pas de voir & d'en lire les Inscriptions. L'endroit où se fait le Service est assez singulier remarquez en l'Autel, & les Tapisseries. De là vous vous ferez mener au

Parliament-House,
Or House of Lords and House of Commons.

Parliament-House,
ou aux deux Chambres de Parlement.

IT is all that remains of the ancient Royal Palace which was reduced to Ashes in the Time of King *Henry* the Eighth; all that could be preserved makes two large Courts, one of them is called the *Court of Requests*, and lies between the House of Lords and St. *Stephen's* Chapel, or the House of Commons; and

C'Est ce qui est resté de l'ancien Palais des Rois qui fut reduit en Cendres au Tems de Henry VIII. ce qu'on en a conservé fait deux grandes Sales dont l'une s'apelle la Cour des Requetes qui est entre la Chambre des Seigneurs & la Chapelle de St. Etienne où s'Assemblent les Communes; & en bas est l'autre

and below is the great Hall, which is called *Westminster Hall*, which we will speak of presently.

When you go into this Building by the West-end you find on your Right-hand the House of Lords; you must be bareheaded when you enter there, or forfeit Six-pence. You will see at the upper-end of this Room, which is not very large, the Throne, on the Right-side of the same an Arm-Chair for the Prince of *Wales*; and on the Left another for the Duke of *York*. You will also ob-serve the Bar, where the Commons, preceded by their Speaker, attend, when sent for by the Usher of the Black-Rod, who always sits near the Bar on the Right-hand as you go in. There are Forms along the Wall on the Right-hand, whereon the Dukes, Marquisses, and Earls place them-selves according to their Rank and Seniority. On the Left, there are others for the 24 Bishops: And on the middle Forms all

l'autre Grande Salle qu'on appelle Westminster-Hall, dont nous allons parler.

En entrant dans cet En-droit par l'Occident vous trouvez à droite la Cham-bre des Seigneurs ; Il faut se decouvrir en y entrant sous peine de six Sous d'Amende. Vous verrez au haut de cette Chambre qui n'est pas fort grande, le Throne, & au coté Droit, un fauteuil pour le Prince de Galles, & au Gauche un autre fauteuil pour le Duc d'York. Vous remarquerez aussi la Barre, ou les Communes precedees de leur Orateur se rendent, lors qu'ils y sont mandés par l'huisier de la Verge-Noire, lequel s'assied tou-jours proche de la Barre à Droite en Entrant. Il y a des Bancs le long de la Muraille du même coté où les Ducs les Marquis & les Comtes se placent selon leur Rang & Ancienneté. A Gauche il y en a un pour les 24 Eveques ; & sur ceux du Milieu sont assis tous les autres Seig=neurs

C

the other have their Seats; but they have immediately before them at the upper end, the Clerks of the House, and on each side the 12 Judges, who sit upon Wool-Packs, to remind them (as 'tis said) in their giving their Opinions, that the Woollen Manufactury ought to be preferr'd to all the other Interests and Advantages of *England*. Before the Throne is a great Form, whereon the Lords Justices are seated, when they are obliged to assemble the Parliament during the King's Absence; and behind the Throne there is a little Form where the Peers eldest Sons may sit, in order to instruct themselves of the Affairs of the Nation when they hear them debated in that august Senate. The Two Arch-bishops of *Canterbury* and *York* are seated by themselves on a little Form on the right hand of the Throne near a Chimney that is between them and the Bishops. Behind the House of Lords there is the

neurs, mais ils ont immediatement devant eux les Secretaires ou Greffiers de la Chambre, & des deux cotez sont assis les 12 Juges sur de Sacs de Laine, afin qu'ils se souviennent (à ce qu'on dit) dans leurs Decisions, que la Manufacture des Laines est à preferer à tous les autres Interets & Biens de l'*Angleterre*. Devant le Throne il y a un Grand Banc où les Regents du Royaume s'asseyent lors qu'on est obligé de convoquer le Parlement durant l'Absence du Roy; & derriere le Throne il y a un petit Banc où les Fils Ainés des Seigneurs peuvent s'asseoir afin de s'instruire des Affaires de la Nation, en les entendant traiter dans cette Auguste Senat. Les deux Archeveques de *Cantorbery* & d'*York*, sont places à Part sur un petit Banc à la droite du Throne proche d'une Cheminée qui est entre eux & les Eveques. Il y a derriere la Chambre des Seigneurs celle où les Souverains se

the King's Robing Room where the Sovereign puts on his Regal Garments before he comes into the House of Lords; and there are other Apartments where the Lords put on their Scarlet Robes lin'd with Ermines, on the Days when the King comes to the Parliament. Behind the Entry through which the King goes to the Parliament there is a little Court, through which the Conspirators had a mind to blow up King *James* I. and his Parliament, by means of the Gunpowder and Fagots they had fill'd a neighbouring Vault with, which was directly under the Parliament; at the Door of which one *Guy Faux a Roman* Catholick Gentleman, was taken with a Dark-Lanthorn in his hand; a House has since been built before it, in order to prevent the like Attempts for the future. The Hangings in the House of Lords represent *Philip* II. Fleet call'd the *Invincible Armado,* but was destroy'd by Queen *Elizabeth;* the *Hollanders*

and

revetent de leurs Habits Royaux avant d'entrer dans la Chambre des Seigneurs; & il y a d'autres Apartemens où les Seigneurs s'habillent de leur Robes Ecarlate fourrées d'Ermines lorsque le Roy doit se trouver au Parlement. Derriere l'Entrée par où le Roy monte au Parlement est une petite Cour par où les Conjurés de la Conspiration des Poudres devoient faire sauter en l'air le Roi Jaques I. & son Parlement par le Moyen d'une Voute qui étoit directement au dessous ils avoient remplie de Fagots la quelle de Poudre, &c. & a la sortie de la quelle l'un d'eux nommé Guy Faux, Gentilhomme, Catholique Romain, fut pris avec une Lanterne sourde a la Main or au devant de cette voute on a depuis batit une Maison pour prevenir de parriel desseins u l'avenir. Les Tapisseries dont la Chambre des Seigneurs est Tendue Representent la flotte de Philipe II. appellée l'Invincible, mais qui fut Entierement detruite par la

C 2

Reine

and the Storms. Coming out of the House of Lords you come into a spacious Hall, call'd the *Court of Requests*; during the Sessions of Parliament it is fill'd with the Members of both Houses, and others, who meet there to talk about Business. There are also Coffee-Houses and Shops at the end of this Hall. Towards the East you find a Stair-Case that brings you up to the

Reine Elizabeth, *les Hollandois & les Tempetes.* En sortant de la Chambre des Seigneurs vous entrés dans une Grande Salle qu'on appelle la Cour des Requetes; durant la séance du Parlement cette Salle est remplie de Membres des deux Chambres, & autres personnes qui s'y rendent pour parler d'Affaires. Il y a aussi au bout de cette Salle des des Coffé & Boutiques. A Droite en allant vers l'Orient vous trouvés un Escalier qui vous mene a la

Chapel of St. Stephen.

Chapelle de St. Étienne.

Wherein the Members of the House of Commons meet, they are 558 in Number, but were never there altogether at the same time: There is nothing very remarkable in this famous House, excepting that the most august Senate in the Universe meets there. Going down the same Stairs by which you went up to the House of Commons, you find another, which you go down also, and which

C'est là que les Membres de la Chambre des Communes s'assemblent, ils sont au nombre de 558 mais ils ne s'y sont jamais trouvés tous en meme tems: il n'y a rien de fort remarquable dans cette fameuse Chambre excepte que le plus auguste Senat de l'Univers s'y Assemble. En decendant le meme Degre par le quel vous etes monte a la Chambre des Communes, vous en trouvez un autre que vous descendez aussi

which brings you to a dark Passage, thro' which you come into

& qui vous mène par un Passage assez obscur, à la

Westminster-Hall.

Westminster-Hall.

ON the Left-hand as you enter in it you find the *King's-Bench* Court; next to that is the Court of *Chancery*. On each side of the Hall there are Shops, and on the Left towards the East is the Court of *Common-Pleas.* Take notice of the Roof of this Hall, which is made of *Irish* Oak, and whereon, for that reason, no Spider is ever seen. Round this Hall are the Standards and Colours taken from the *French* by the Duke of *Marlborough* at the Battle of *Hocksted.* There is also a fine Head of King *Charles* I. Then going forwards you find on the Left a Stair that leads to the Court of *Exchequer,* of which the L. Treasurer is Chancellor, having under him four Judges, called *Barons of the Exchequer.* It is in this Hall that the Feast is

EN y entrant vous trou-vez a Gauche le Tribunal de la Cour du Banc du Roy; tout a coté est celui de la Cour de la Chancelerie. A chaque cotés il y a des Boutiques, & en allant au haut de la Sale vers l'Orient, vous trouvez a Gauche celui de la Cour des Plaidoyers Communs. Remarquez bien la Voute de cette Sale, qui est faite & supportée de Bois de Chêne d'Irlande, & où par cette raison là il ne se loge jamais A'raignée. Au haut de cette Sale vous verrez tout à l'Entour les Drapeaux & Etendars, qui ont été pris sur les François par le Duc de Marlborough à la Battaille de Hockster. Il y a aussi une belle Tete de Charles I. Dela vous a-vancez & trouvez a Gauche un Escalier qui mène a la Cour de l'Echiquier où des Aides dont le Sur-Intendant des Finances est Chancelier,

C 3

ayant

is made after the Coronation, and where the King dines with all the Peers of the Kingdom.

As the Peers of *England* and *Scotland*, are not oblig'd to submit themselves to any Judicature for Crimes by them committed, unless it be to the Judgment of their Peers, when any of them is to be Try'd, a Scaffold is erected in this Great Hall at the King's Charge, in which (in Presence of the Lord High Steward, created only for that Tryal) all the Peers having heard the Depositions, judge him, and acquit, or condemn him, by saying, *Guilty upon my Honour*, or *Not Guilty upon my Honour*. And the High Steward passes Sentence according to the majority of Votes, and then breaks his Staff, and that puts an end to his Trust.

Besides these Curiosities there is nothing remarkable to be seen at *Westminster*. On certain Holy

ayant sous lui quatre *[...]* nommés Barons de l'Echiquier. C'est dans cette Salle que se fait le Regal après le Couronnement, & où le Roi Dine avec tous les Pairs du Royaume.

Comme les Pairs d'Angleterre, & d'Ecosse ne sont point obligé de se soumettre à aucune Judicature pour Crimes par eux Commis, sinon au Jugement de Pairie, lors qu'on peut faire le Procés à quelqu'un d'eux on erige un Batiment dans la Grande Salle, aux dépens du Roy; dans lequel (en Presence du Grand Senechal créé pour ce seulement) tous les Seigneurs ayant ouï les Depositions, le Jugent, & l'absolvent ou le condamnent en disant, Coupable sur mon Honneur, ou Non Coupable sur mon Honneur, & le Senechal lui Pronionce sa Sentence selon la majorité des Voix & casse sa Baguete & cela termine sa Charge.

Il n'y a outre ceci rien de Remarquable à voir à Westminster. A certaines Fêtes aux quelles

Holy-days on which the Parliament is obliged to go in a Body to hear Divine Service, the Lords go to the Abby of *West-minster*, and the Commons to St. *Margaret*'s Church, which is hard by, and which you may see if you please.

After you have seen all these Places, you return by *King-street*, and passing before *Whitehal*, and the Horse-Guard, you will see the *Admiralty-Office*, which is newly rebuilt, and is a very magnificent and large Edifice. Thence you come to *Charing-Cross*, which is a Triangle, where King *Charles* the First's Statue in Brass is erected, it deserves your particular Notice.

On the East of this Statue is *Northumberland-House*, where the Duke of *Somerset* resides, and which formerly belong'd to the Earls of *Northum-berland*, whose only Heiress the present Duke married. It is a large House, it has fine Walks very well kept, and which re-

le *Parlement* est obligé d'aller en Corps assister au Service Divin, les Seigneurs vont a l'Abbaye de *Westminster*, & les Communes a l'Eglise de Ste. *Marguerite*, qui en est tout proche. Or que vous pourrez voir s'il vous plait.

Après avoir vu ces Curiosités vous reprenez par *King-street* & passant devant *Whitehal*, & la Garde a Cheval, vous verrez l'Hotel de l'Admiraute, qu'on a nouvellement Rebati, & qui est un tres magnifique Edifice. De la vous venez a *Charing-Cross*, qui est un Triangle, ou est la Statue equestre de *Charles* Premier, qui merite votre attention.

A l'Orient de cette Statue est l'Hotel de Nor-thumberland, ou le Duc de *Somerset* fait sa Residence & qui appartenoit aux Comtes de Northumberland, dont le present Duc a Epousé l'unique Heritiere. C'est un vaste Hotel qui a de belles Allées qui sont tres bien entre-tenues

terminate to the *Thames.* Then you'll go to the *Mews,* which you'll be surpriz'd to hear are the King's Stables, tho' they only serve now as such to their Royal Highnesses the Prince and Princess of *Wales.* The Horse and Grenadier Guards Parade there when they mount the Guard. And there is is also a Riding School, where every Morning they learn to Ride. Thence you'll go up to the Street, and entring in the second Street on your Left, you will come to *Leicester-Fields,* where is *Leicester-House,* which with another House annexed to it make

tenuës se terminent a la Thamise. *De là vous vous ferez mener dans la Meuse, ou vous serez surpris d'apprendre que ce sont les Ecuries du Roy, quoi qu'a present Elles servent Principalement à Leurs Altesses Royales le Prince & la Princesse de Galles. Les Gardes du Corps s'y assemblent lorsqu'ils vont monter la Garde aussi bien que les Grenadiers à Cheval. Et y font le manège tous les Matins. De là vous Monterez la Ruë & en entrant dans la seconde Ruë a Gauche vous viendrez à* Leicester-Fields, *où est* Leicester-House, *qui avec un autre Hotel qu'on y a joint, compose*

The Palace of Leicester,

Le Palais de Leicester,

WHere His Royal Highness the Prince of *Wales* keeps his Court. This Palace is situated on the North of a fine Square environ'd with Pales, which contain a Green-Plot that makes a very good Prospect

OU *son Altesse Royale Monseigneur le Prince de Galles tient sa Cour. Ce Palais est situé au Nord d'un beau Quarré environné de Pallissades, qui renferment un Parterre qui fait un tres bel Effet. Le Palais n'est pas Extraordinaire*

spect. This Palace is not Extraordinary, notwithstanding the Additions and Improvements His Royal Highness has made to it; but you must observe, it was only the House of the Earl of *Leicester:* But what makes fully amends for this is, the most kind and extraordinary Gracious and Noble Deportment of His Royal Highness the Prince of *Wales,* and the Affability and ingaging Sweetness, *&c.* of Her Royal Highness the Princess, with which all those who have the Honour to approach Her, are at once dazled, surprised and charmed. The young Princesses, and the young Prince *William* are also the Objects of the Love and Admiration of this Nation, together with Prince *Frederick,* whom this Nation (on the excellent Character given of him by all who have had the Honour to see him) long to have among them. And those Illustrious Offsprings brought up under the

ordinaire non obstant les Additions & les Embellissements que son Altesse Royale y a fait; mais on doit remarquer que ce n'etoit auparavant que l'Hotel du Comte de Leicester *; en revanche on sera Charmé des Manieres remplies de Bonté & Extraordinairement Gracieuses de son Altesse Royale Monseigneur le Prince de* Galles, *& de l'affabilité & engageante Douceur,* &c. *de Madame la Princesse, dont Personne n'a l'Honneur d'approcher, sans en etre tout a la fois Ebloui, Surpris, & Charmé. Les Princesses & le Jeune Prince leurs Enfans font aussi l'Amour & l'Admiration de cette Nation; aussi bien que le Prince* Frederick, *que les peuples des cette Nation (sur l'excellent Caractere que lui donnent tous ceux qui ont eu l'honneur de le voir) languissent d'avoir parmi eux. Et ces Illustres Rejetons, Elevé sous les Yeux de leur Auguste Ayeul, & de leurs Altess Roy-*

the Care of their august Grandfather and their Royal Highnesses, give us reason to hope that they will make it, after those Royal Patterns, a happy, dreaded, and flourishing People.

Thence you'll go to the Church of St. *Martin in the Fields*, which is the Royal Parish. It is very fine, and together with its Steeple, are of an excellent Taste of Architecture.

You'll go afterwards and see *York-Buildings*, whose fine Gate to the River is extraordinary. This is one of the cleanest Places in *London*.

From thence you will go through *Round-Court* into *Covent-Garden*, where is kept a publick Market for Pot and Physick Herbs, &c. observe St. *Paul's* Church there, which is reckon'd a Master-piece of Architecture, and view the Inside of it. Hard by the Church and at the end of the Piazzas, is the Earl of *Oxford's* House, he is better known by the Name

Royales, ont lieu de se flatter de l'Esperance que ces Illustres Rejettons les rendront à l'Imitation de ces Augustes Exemples, un Peuple redoutable, heureux & florissant.

De la vous irez voir l'Eglise de St. *Martin* des Prés, qui est la Paroisse Royale. Elle est tres belle & est, aussi bien que le Clocher d'un excellent Goust d'Architecture.

Vous irez ensuite voir York-Building, dont vous admirerez le Beau Portail sur la Riviere. C'est un des plus propres Endroit de Londres.

De la vous irez par Round-Court au Commun Jardin, où un Marché publick pour toutes sortes d'Herbes Potageres ou Medicinales, &c. & des Arcades. Vous y remarquerez l'Eglise de St. Paul, qui passe pour un chef d'oeuvre d'Architecture, & dont vous devez aussi voir l'Interieur, & tout près de l'Eglise, & au bout des Arcades la Maison du Comte d'Oxford plus connu sous le Nom

Name of Admiral *Ruffel*, who in 1692. defeated Admiral *de Tourville* near *la Hogue*, and ruined the *French* Fleet.

From *Covent-Garden* you may go by *South-hampton-ftreet* to the *Strand*, where you may, if you pleafe, fee the two *Exchanges*, where all manner of Goods are fold.

Going on to the Eaft, you come on your Right hand to the ancient Palace of *Lancafter*, now called

Nom d'Amiral Ruffel qui defit en 1692. l'Amiral Tourville au Combat de la Hogue, & ruina la Flotte de France.

De la vous irez par la Ruë de Southampton dans le Strand ou vous verrez, fi vous voulez les deux Bourfes ou il y a des Marchands qui vendent toutes fortes de Curiofités.

En allant vers l'Orient vous trouvez à droit l'ancien Palais de Lancaftre qu'on appelle à prefent

The *Savoy*,

La Savoye,

FRom its Founder *Peter* Count of *Savoy* and Earl of *Richmond*, Uncle to *Eleanor* Spoufe to *Henry* III. which *Henry* bought it from the faid Earl of *Savoy* for his Son *Edmund* Duke of *Lancafter*. But it is now fallen to Ruins, and nothing remains of it but the antient Chapel, and fome old Remains, on the *Thames*. It was in one of thefe old Houfes that King

DE fon fondateur Pierre Comte de Savoye & de Richmond, Oncle d'Eleonore *Femme de* Henry III. lequel Henry l'acheta enfuite du dit Comte de Savoye pour fon Fils Edmund Duc de Lancafter. Mais il eft à prefent tombé en Ruines & il n'en refte que l'ancienne Chapelle & quelques Mafures qui font fur le Bord de la Thamife, & c'eft dans une des

King *John* of *France* was lodged when this Palace was his Prison: That Prince died in *England*. There are in this Place an *English*, a *French*, and two *German* Churches, one *Calvinist* the other *Lutheran*, and a Meeting of Quakers. The Prison of the Provost-Marshal of the Army is near the *English* Chapel, as also some Cazerns for a Batallion of Foot Guards. A great Passage has lately been made there, for the Coaches which go to the *German* Chapel, and a Church-yard lately wall'd up there.

Going out of the *Savoy* towards the East, you come directly into

Somerset-House.

IT was built by the Duke of *Somerset*, who was Protector of the Kingdom during the Minority of King *Edward* VI. his Nephew. It is a large Palace, but so ill contriv'd within, that it

---

des *Maisons qui y sont que Jean Roy de France*, fut *Logé lors qu'on lui donna ce Palais pour Prison*. Ce *Prince mourut en Angleterre*. *Il y a dans cet endroit une Eglise Angloise, une Françoise, deux Allemandes, l'une Calviniste & l'autre Lutherienne, & une Assemblée de Quacres. Proche de la Chapelle, est la Prison du Grand Provost & tout proche de là il y a des Casernes pour un Bataillon des Gardes à Pieds. On y a depuis peu pratiqué une grande Allée pour les Carosses qui decendent a l'Eglise Alemande de & a un Cimetiere qu'on a nouvellement environné de Murailles.*

Au sortir de là allant vers l'Orient vous entrez directement au

Somerset-House.

IL fut bati par le Duc de *Somerset*, qui fut *Protecteur du Royaume durant la Minorité du jeune Roy Edward VI. son Neveu. C'est un vaste Palais, mais si mal Construit au dedans qu'il paroit*

it very plainly appears the Architects of those Days had no great Skill. As you go down towards the Garden you will see dark Stairs, and Passages, and lower Courts, that looks more like those of a Prison than of a Palace. The back Front towards the *Thames* is more Regular: And the Garden, in which there is a very spacious Bowling-green, is very agreeable, and has a fine Prospect. Several Persons of Quality and others are lodged therein by Favour. This Palace is commonly the Place where the Queen Dowagers reside, *Catherine* of *Portugal*, Dowager to K. *Charles* II. was the last who kept her Court there.

Thence, going towards the City, you see the New Church in the *Strand*, which is of singular Beauty, but little, and too much expos'd to the rattling of Coaches, which hinders the hearing of Divine Service plain enough therein.

paroit bien que les Architectes de ce tems là n'etoient pas fort habiles. Vous y trouverez en descendant pour aller au Jardin des Escaliers & des Passages fort sombres & des basses Cours qui ressemblent plutot a celles d'une Prison qu'a celles d'un Palais. Le derriere qui donne sur la Thamise est plus Regulier, et le Jardin dans lequel il y a deux Boulingrins fort spacieux est fort agreable, & a une tres belle Vuë. Plusieurs Personnes de Qualité & autres y sont Logés par Faveur. Ce Palais est ordinairement le Lieu de la Residence des Reines Douairieres, Catherine de Portugal, Douairiere du Roy Charles II. est la derniere qui y a tenu sa Cour.

De là en remontant vers la Ville vous voyez l'Eglise de St. Marie dans le Strand, qui est d'une Beauté singuliere mais petite & trop exposé au Bruit des Carosses, ce qui fait qu'on n'y peut bien entendre le Service Divin.

A

A little further to the East you come to the Church of St. *Clement Danes*, thus called because the *Danes* had a Church-yard there formerly. The Architecture of this is one of the best in *London*. You come a little farther East to the Gate called

Temple-Bar,

ON which you see the Statues of King *Charles* I. and King *Charles* II. his Son; and on the inside those of *Philip* II. of *Spain* and of Queen *Mary* of *England* his Spouse.

Turning to the Right a little higher you come into the *Temple*, so called because it was formerly the place of Residence of the *Knights Templars*; but it is now that of a great number of Barifters and Lawyers. This *Temple*, which is very large, is divided into *Inner* and *Middle-Temple*; it contains several very handsome Courts, where there

Un peu plus haut vers l'Orient on trouve l'Eglise de St. Clement *les Danois, ainsi nommée parce que les* Danois *y avoient autrefois un Cimetiere. L'Architecture de cette Eglise est des Meilleures de* Londre. *Ensuite vous venez à la Porte dite*

Temple-Bar,

SUr laquelle vous voyez les Statues de Charles *I. & de* Charles *II. son Fils, & en dedans celles de* Philipe *II. d'Espagne, & de la Reine* Marie *d'Angleterre son Epouse.*

Et en détournant à droite quelques Pas de là vous entrez dans le Temple, *ainsi appellé par ce que c'étoit autrefois la Résidence des Chevaliers Templiers; mais c'est aujourd'huy celle d'un grand Nombre de Jurisconsultes & Etudiant en Droit. Ce* Temple *qui est fort spacieux se divise en Temple-Interieur & en Temple du Milieu. Il contiennent plusieurs Cours fort*

there are fine Buildings and Walks, and a great wide Place where People walk, and from most of which you have a Prospect of the River, each of these have their Library and Dining-Hall, where the Lawyers pay a certain Sum to Dine during the Terms, that is to say, the four Times of the Year the Courts sit at *Westminster.* You must not fail to see the Chapel which is very fine, and in which you see, besides other Tombs, &c. the Tombs of eleven *Knights-Templars.* This Place is Privileged, and one cannot be arrested for Debt in the *Temple.*

From thence you go into *Fleetstreet,* and go as far as *Fleet-Ditch,* which is a Canal made by Q. *Elizabeth,* and all along the same are Vaults where they keep the Sea-Cole that is brought from the great Cole-Mines near *Newcastle.* Going down this Ditch on your Right Hand you find the Hospital of *Bridewel,* which is a House of Correction where-

fort propres, où il y a de beaux Edifices, de Belles Promenades qui donnent presque toutes sur la Riviere, une & grande Place où l'on se promene. Chacun a sa Chapelle, ses Bibliotheques, & sa Salle à Manger, où les Avocats payent tant par Tête durant les Termes, c'est à dire quatre Tems de l'année où l'on tient les Cours des Plaidoyers à *Westminster.* Vous ne devez pas manquer de voir la Chapelle qui est très-belle, & où outre les autres Tombeaux, &c. on voit ceux d'Onze Chevaliers Templiers. Cet endroit est Privilègié, & on ne peut y être Arrêté pour Dettes.

De là vous remontez dans la *Fleet-street,* & vous venez jusqu'à *Fleet-Ditch,* qui est un Canal fait par la Reine *Elizabeth,* tout le long duquel il y a des voutes où on garde le Charbon de Terre qu'on brule en cette Ville & qu'on y apporte des grandes Mines qui sont près de *Newcastle.* En descendant le long de ce Canal à Droite vous trouves l'Hopital de *Bridewel,* qui est une

wherein every Fortnight Correction is given to the loose Fellows or Women who are confined there for Thefts, Debaucheries, or loose Pranks, or for not being assiduous with, or obedient to their Masters; they beat Hemp here all the Week, and there are some who remain here much longer than the Time they are condemn'd to stay, for want of Money to pay the Fees, or Dues of the House: but there are charitable Persons who discharge them, from time to time.

Crossing over the Bridge which is against *Bridewel*, you come into *Black-Fryars*, where formerly was a Monastery of Black Fryars, and where there is nothing worth your notice except the Apothecaries Hall and the Royal Printing-House. But if you return from *Bridewel* towards *Fleet-street* you go then towards the City, and you'll come to *Ludgate*, on which Gate you'll see the Statue of the

une Maison de Correction où l'on fait tous les 15 jours Justice de tous les Garnemens, &c. Vaux rien qui y sont detenus pour Larcins, Debauces, Libertinages, ou pour n'etre point assidus & obeïsans à leurs Maitres ; on leur fait battre du Chanvre toute la Semaine, & il y en a qui y restent plusque le tems à quoi ils sont condamnés faute d'avoir dequoi payer les fraix, ou Droits de la Maison. Mais il y a des Gens fort Charitables qui les en retirent de tems en tems.

En passant sur le Pont vis à vis de Bridewel, vous entrez dans les Black-Fryars, où il y avoit autrefois un Monastere de Moines Noirs, & où il n'y a rien de remarquable sinon la Halle des Apothiquaires & l'Imprimerie Royale. Mais si vous retournez de Bridewel, vers la grande Ruë vous montez vers la Ville, & vous trouvez la Porte de Ludgate, sur la quelle on voit la Statue de la fameuse Reine Elisabeth.

the famous Queen *Eli-zabeth*, and on the Inside, those of *Lud*, King of the *Britons*, and of *Androgeus* and *Theomantius* his Sons and Successors. This Gate, and a great Building adjoining to it, is a Prison for the Freemen of *London* only, who cannot be arrested under 40 Shillings. They are for the most part maintained with the Charities that are given them. Then going up this Street, you see before you the

Cathedral of St. Paul's.

WHich is the only Metropolitan in *Europe*, that is dedicated to that Saint.

This Church, for Amplitude, Splendor, Solidity, Figure, and curious Architecture, is esteemed the first in all the Universe; it is built of fine *Portland* Stone, Rustick-work, adorn'd with above 300 Pilasters in 2 Ranges, and other curious Enrichments.

& en de dans celles de Lud Roy des Bretons, & d'Androgeus & Theomantius ses Fils & Successeurs. Cette porte & un Grand Batiment qui y joint est la Prison de ceux qui sont Freemen de Londres, c'est à dire qui y ont droit de Maitrise & qu'on ne peut arreter à moins de 40 Shillings, ou huit Ecus; ils y sont la plus part nourry des Charités qu'on leur fait. En montant cette Rue vous voyez devant vous la

Cathedrale de St. Paul.

QUi est la seule Metropolitaine de l'Europe qui soit dedite à ce Saint.

Cette Eglise est estimée la priemiere de tous le Univers pour sa grandeur, sa Magnificence, sa Solidité, sa Figure, & sa belle Architecture ; elle est batie de belle Pierre de taille, d'ouvrage Rustique orné de plus de 300 Piliers en 2 rangs & autres ouvrages curieux. On

D   *monte*

ments. The Ascent to the three Doors, are by large graceful Steps; the Porticoes of which are supported by spacious Columns. The whole Church is surrounded with Iron Rails, and at the West Entrance of it, you will see the Statue of Queen *Anne* in Marble (and in a modern Dress) upon a Pedestal also of Marble, having four Statues seated on each Angle of the Pedestal, representing the four Nations of *Great-Britain, Ireland*, and *America*, which you may easily distinguish by the Shield of their Arms, which they hold in their Hands. Above the Frontispiece, which is of an exquisite Workmanship and Taste, and in the Pediment, the Conversion of St. *Paul* is very well represented. That Saint is above the Pediment, and the twelve Apostles and others round the Church. When you have observed the outward Beauties, enter into the Church, and follow the great Nave which leads

monte aux 3 portes par de grandes et belles Marches couvertis de Portiques soutenus de grosse Colomnes. Toute la place de l'Eglise est environnée d'une balustrade de fer d'un fer bel ouvrage, & a l'Entrée du coté du Couchant, vous voyez d'abord la Statuë de la Reine Anne en Marbre, & à la Moderne sur un Pied d'Estal, aussi de Marbre & ayant quatre Statues assise une a Chaque Angle du Pied d'Estal, representant les quatre Nations de la Grande-Bretagne, d'Irlande, & d'Amerique, que vous distinguerez aisément par l'Ecu de leurs Armes qu'elles ont a la Main; au haut du Frontispice qui est d'un Goût Exquis & sur le Fronton, vous voyez tres bien representée la Conversion de St. Paul. Ce Saint est aussi bien que les Douze Apotres au dessus de l'Eglise lors que vous aurez bien. Remarqué les Beautez du dehors entre dans l'Eglise & suivez la Grande Nef qui mene vers le Choeur, & vous verrez

au

leads to the Quire, and before you come to it you see on the Top of the Cupola, all the History of that Great Apostle of the *Gentiles* Painted by Sir *James Thornhill.* Afterwards you'll see the Quire, the Ornaments and Sculpture of which are extraordinary Fine: Then go above to the Gallery of the Cupola, from whence you will much better observe the abovesaid Painting, and where leaning your Head against the Wall, you may easily hear all that is said, tho' it be whisper'd ever so low and at the most distant Place from you in the same Gallery. Go afterwards to the Top of the Cupola on the outside, thence (if it be fair Weather) you may agreeably observe the immense largeness of the Town, the vast number of Churches and publick Buildings, the great number of Ships, Vessels, and Boats on the *Thames,* and the fine Country round about. In short, I doubt not but you

au haut du *Dome* toute l'*Histoire* de la Vie de ce *Grand Apotre des Gentils* peinte par le *Chevalier Thornhill.* Ensuite vous verrez le *Choeur,* dont les *Ornemens* & la *Sculpture* font tres beaux. De là montez sur les voutes & faites vous mener dans la *Gallerie* du *Dome* d'ou vous remarquerez bien mieux la *Peinture* susdite, & où en mettant la *Tete* contre la *Muraille* on entend facilement tout ce qui s'y dit, quand même on le prononceroit aussi bas qu'il seroit possible, a l'*Endroit* de la même *Gallerie* le plus eloigne de vous. Montez ensuite jusqu'au haut du *Dome,* d'où vous observeriez avec *Plaisir* (s'il fait beau Tems.) l'*Immense Grandeur* de la *Ville,* la vaste quantité d'*Eglises,* & d'*Edifices Publics,* & le grand nombre de *Vaisseaux, Barques* & *Bateaux* sur la *Thamise.* Enfin je ne doute point que vous n'avouiez que c'est là plus *Belle Vue* de l'*Univers. Faites* vous

D 2   ensuite

you will own it is the finest Prospect in the Universe. Go next to see the Mathematical Marble Stairs, and see the Model of this Church and of St. *Peter's* at *Rome*. Go after this to see the Vaults under the Church, to admire the Largeness and Solidity of the same, and let them shew you the Tombs that are there. You must pay six Pence to see the Cupola, three Pence to see the Stairs, three Pence to see the Model, and three Pence to see the Vaults.

This Church is built upon the most eminent Place of the City; and 'tis said that when they laid the Foundation of the Cathedral that was Burnt at the great Fire of *London*, they found there the Bones of Oxen and other Victims, that had been Sacrificed to *Diana*, to whom the Heathen Temple that was built in this Place, was Consecrated. It is observable, that this Cathedral, which was near fourty Years a Building, and

ensuite conduire à l'Escalier (de Marbre) suspendu & voyez le Modele de l'Eglise & celui de St. Pierre de Rome; et ensuite allez voir les voutes de dessous pour en remarquer la Grandeur & la Solidité, et faites vous montres les Tombeaux qui y sont. On paye six Sols pour voir le Dôme, 3 Sols pour voir l'Escalier suspendu, 3 Sols pour voir le Modele, & trois Sols pour voir les voutes de dessous.

Cette Eglise est batie sur l'Endroit le plus Eminent de la Ville, & on dit qu'en posant les fondement de la Cathedrale qui fut brulée dans le Grand Incendie de Londres, on y trouva des Offémens de Boeufs, & autres Victimes qu'on y avoit immolés a Diane, à qui le Temple Payen qui etoit bati dans cet Endroit etoit consacrez. Il est remarquable que cette Cathedrale qui a eté près de 40 ans a Batir & qu'on a Commencé a rebatir en 1675, a eté commencé & finie par le meme Architecte le Chevalier Wren,

and was begun in 1675, was begun and ended by the same Architect, Sir *Christopher Wren*, and by the same Master *Mason*, Mr. *Strong*. The *English* pretend this Cathedral exceeds that of St. *Peters* at *Rome*, in Length, Breadth, and in Excellence of Architecture: We leave it to the Learned, who have seen both, to decide this Dispute.

Going out of this Church, observe the outsides thereof. Go on to the *East*, and through St. *Paul*'s Church-Yard, you come into the fine Street call'd *Cheapside*, where, as well as in all the Streets from *Charing-Cross*, the great Concourse of People, the Magnificence of the Shops and Merchandises, will Surprise and Charm you: When you are passed by the Church of St. *Mary le Bow*, which has a Magnificent Steeple 225 Foot high; there commonly the Bishops are Confirmed; You turn on the left into *King ſtreet*, at the End of which

Wren, & par le même Maître Maçon, Mr. Strong. Les Anglois veulent que cette Cathedrale ſurpaſſe celle de St. Pierre de Rome, en Grandeur, Largeur, et en Excellence d'Architecture; nous laiſſons cela à decider aux Connoiſſeurs qui ont vu l'une & l'autre.

Au Sortir de cette Egliſe remarquez en tous les de-hors & par le Cimetiere de St. Paul vous allez vers l'Eſt, entrez dans la Belle Rue qu'on appelle Cheapſide, où comme par toute la Grande l'Affluence du Monte & la Magnificence des Boutiques & Marchandiſes, a tout a la fois dequoi Surprendre & Charmer. Lors qu's vous aurez paſſez l'Egliſe de Ste. Marie le Bow, qui a un Magnifique Clocher qui a 225 Pieds de haut; & où p,ur l'Ordinaire on confirme les Evêques, vous detournerez a Gauche & entrerez dans King-Street, au bout de la quelle eſt Guild-Hall, où la Maiſon

de

which is *Guild-Hall*, or the *Town-House*; it is an Ancient Building, where the Livery Men (who are the only ones, who have the Right in this City, to Vote for the Election of Mayors, Sheriffs, Chamberlain, Members of Parliament) meet to Elect them; they amount to about eight or nine Thousand, and if all the Freemen had Votes, they would amount to above 150,000, which ought to seem prodigious, since of ten Housekeepers of this City, there are not above four who are Freemen of the City. You'll see there two Giants above the great Stairs which faces the Entry; they give out that these Giants were of the Race of the first Inhabitants of this Island; which shews that all Nations have endeavour'd to find something fabulous to raise themselves by, something or other above their Neighbouring Nations: Though it is certain, this

de *Ville*; c'est un Ancien Edifice où les Bourgeois Jurés qui sont les Seuls de cette *Ville* qui ont droit de donner leurs Suffrages pour les Elections de Maire, Echevins, Chambellan, & Membres de Parlement s'assemblent pour les leur donner. Ils se montent a environ huit a neuf Mille, & si tous les Bourgeois ayant Maitrise avoient Suffrages il y en auroit plus de 150 Mille, ce qui doit sembler prodigieux, puis que de dix Bourgeois de cette *Ville* & fauxbourgs on n'en compte par plus de quatre qui ayent Maitrise dans la Cité. Vous y remarquerez deux Géants au dessus de l'Escalier qui fait face a l'entrée, on dit que ces Géants etoient de la Race des premiers habitans de cette *Isle*, ce qui fait voir que toutes les Nations ont Voulu trouver dans la fable dequoi S'elever par quelque Endroit au dessus des Nations Circonvoisines; quoi qu'il soit certain que cette *Isle* a eté premierement Peuplée par les Gaulois comme on le peut voir par des Commentaires *de*

this Island was Peopled by the *Gauls*, as may be seen by *Cæsar's* Commentaries, and a Number of other Proofs. There is nothing very Curious in this Building, but you must observe the Picture of Queen *Anne* in her Regal Garments, as well as those of King *William*, Queen *Mary*, and King *George*, which is very well done; and round this Hall, those of the Judges of the *King's Bench*. Above these Pictures hang several Standards and Colours, taken from the *French* by the Duke of *Marlborough* at *Ramilies*. It is also in this Hall, that the Lord Mayor and the Court of Aldermen, with the Common-Council meet; these can make City Laws, and oblige all the Citizens to submit thereto; and there are Laws thus made, which have subsisted above 300 Years. The Sheriffs keep also their Court here, wherein they decide and return the Pannels of the Juries.

de *Cæsar* & une Infinité d'autres preuves. Il n'y a rien de remarquable dans cet Edifice, mais vous y devïez observer le Portrait de la Reine *Anne* dans ses habits Royaux, aussi bien que le Roy *Guillaume*, la Reine *Marie*, & de Roy *George* qui est très bien representé; & tout a l'Entour de la Sale ceux des Juges de la Cour du Banc du Roy. Au dessus de ces Portraits pendent divers Drapeaux Enseignes pris sur les *François* par le Duc de *Marlborough* a *Ramilies*. C'est aussi dans cette Maison de Ville que s'Assemble le Lord Maire & la Cour des Aldermen, qui avec les Conseillors de la Ville peuvent faire des Loix Municipales qui obligent tous les habitans de la Cité de s'y soumettre; & il y a des Loix ainsi faites qui subsistent depuis plus de 300 Ans. Les Sheriffs y tiennent aussi leur Cour dans la quelle ils decident du Choix des Jurés qu'on appelle Pannels toute Persons qu'on Juge pour Crime ou Procès

a un

Juries. All Persons tryed for any Crime, or Suit of Law, have a Jury of twelve House-Keepers, who decide his Cause after the Charge is given them by the Judge, and when they are sworn they are call'd Juries. It is an extraordinary Privilege, and there are none but the *English* are so judged by their Fellow-Citizens. The Sheriff appoints a certain Number, and the Criminal may eject 36, or more, if he can prove he has just Reasons so to do. It is also in this Hall that the Chamberlain keeps his Court. It is he who Letts the City Land, &c. and who is supreme Judge between the Masters, Journeymen, and Prentices, concerning the Grievances that arise between them. This Magistrate has a very great Power, his Place is Worth near two Thousand Pounds *per Annum.* The Lord Mayor is always Elected out of the Court of the 26 Aldermen, and succeeds commonly according to his Seniority. The Lord Mayor

a un Juré de Douze Bourgeois nommés pour décider sa Cause & comme ils sont sous serment on les nomme Jurés. C'est un privilege Extraordinaire, & il n'y a que les Anglois qui soient ainsi Jugés par leurs Concitoyens. Le Sheriff a le Droit d'en nommer un Nombre, & le Criminel en peut recuser jusqu'à 36, & même davantage, s'il peut prouver qu'il a de juste Raisons de le faire. C'est aussi dans cet Endroit que le Chambellan de le Ville tient sa Cour. C'est lui qui Loue à ferme les Terres & autre Revenus de la Ville, & qui decide Souverainement entre les Maitres, les Ouvriers & Apprentifs des Griefs qui s'elevent entr'eux. Cet Officier a un tres Grand Pouvoir, sa Charge lui rapporte près de deux Mille Livres Sterlin par An. Le Lord Maire s'elit toujours du Corps des 26 Aldermen & il Succede Ordinairement par Seniorité. Le Lord Maire & les Aldermen choisissent seul le Recorder, qui est leur Juge Assesseur, leur Principal

or and Aldermen chuse the Recorder, who is their Judge, their Speaker, and their Counsellor. The Lord Mayor has the Power to dispose of the Places of Sword-Bearer, Common-Hunt, and others of great Value. His Place and Perquisites are reckoned Worth about 5 or 6000 *l.* per *Annum.* Thus *London* is Governed, by the Mayor, the Aldermen, who, as well as the Common Council Men, are Elected by the Freemen of the Wards they represent, by the two Sheriffs, by the Common Council, by the Chamberlain, and by its Justices of the Peace. It has its own Courts of Judicature and Criminal Court, which is held at the *Old-Bayly* eight times a Year; and lastly, a Water-Bailiff for the River of *Thames,* of which the Lord Mayor is Conservator, from *Sheerness* to *Kingston-Bridge,* which is near 60 Miles.

Going out of *Guild-Hall* you'll return to *Cheapside,* and turning on your left you come to *Mercers-Chapel,*

cipal *Avocat & leur Orateur.* Le Lord Maire a lui seul le pouvoir de Nommer aux Charges de Porte Epée, Chasseurs & autres Charges de Gros & Moindres Revenus. On tient que sa Place & ses Profits reviennent à 5 ou 6000 Livres Sterlins de Rente. Ainsi Londres est Gouverné pour le Maire, par les Aldermen, qui s'elisent aussi bien que les 200 Membres du Conseil de Ville, par les Bourgeois des quartiers où ils sont elu & qu'ils representent, par les 2 Sheriffs, par le Conseil de Ville, par le Chambellan, & par ses Juges a Paix. Elle a ses Cours de Playdoyers & Cour Criminelle, qui si tient au Old Bayly huit fois l'Année; & enfin son Baillif de la Rivierre de la Thamise, dont le Lord Maire est le Conservateur, depuis Sheerness jusqu'au pont de Kingston, ce qui est aprés de 20 Lieuës d'Etenduë.

En sortant de la Maison de Ville vous retournerez dans Cheapside, & en detournant a Gauche vous trouverez la Chapelle des Merciers, qui est tres belle, l'entrée en est spacieuse, & comme on tient

pel, which is very fine, the Entrance into it is spacious, and being used for a Print-Shop, is adorn'd with Pictures, Maps and Prints. And as you go on the same way, you come to *Grocers-Hall*, in which the Bank of *England* is kept. Going on towards the East, you come to one of the City Prisons called the *Compter*; a little higher you come to *Stocks Market*, where there is a Statue of King *Charles* II. on Horseback, trampling an Enemy under his Feet. From thence you enter into *Cornhill*, where you will come to the

tient une *Boutique, d'Imprimez elle se trouve ornée de tailles douces, de Chartes Geographiques, en montant plus haut du Même coté de la vue vous trouverez la Halle des Epiciers dans la quelle est la Banque d'Angleterre. En sortant de la & montant toujours vers l'Orient vous trouvé une des Prison de la Ville nommée le Counter; en montant a quelques pas de la vous trouvez le Marché de* Stock, *ou* Stocks Market, *où il y a une Statue Equestre de Charles II. foulant un Ennemi à ses Pieds. En montant plus haut vous entrez dans* Cornhill *ou vous trouvez la*

Royal Exchange.

Bourse Royale.

IT is a Magnificent Building that was erected at the Expence of the Merchants of the City; it is a square Figure, but 42 foot Longer than Broad, being 203 foot Long from North to South, and 161 foot Broad from East to West. It is wholly built of *Portland* Freestone, and of

C'Est un *Magnifique Edifice qui a été bâti aux Depens des Merchands; elle est d'une Figure quarrée Longue ayant 203 Pieds de Long de l'Orient à l'Occident; sur 161 Pieds de Large du Nord au Sud. Elle est toute batie de Pierre de Taille de* Portland, *& d'une Architecture très belle*

of a very fine and regular Architecture. Its Steeple is extraordinary fine, and the Chime of Bells in it is one of the best in *London*. When you enter it from *Cornhill* you see in a Niche on each side of the Gate, the Statue of K. *Charles* I. and K. *Charles* II. When you come within the Exchange you perceive immediately the Statue of *Charles* II. in Marble, and the *Latin* Inscription following, upon it.

Carolo Secundo, *Cæsari Britannico, Patriæ Patri, Regum Optimo, Clementissimo, Augustissimo, Generis Humani Deliciis, Utriusque Fortunæ Victori Pacis Europæ Arbitro, Maris Domino & vindici.*

Societas Mercatorum Adventur. Angliæ, *quæ per* CCCC *jam Annos Regia Benignitate floret, Fidei intemeratæ & Gratitudinis Æternæ, hoc Testimonium venerabundæ posuit,* Anno Salutis 1684.

This is,

Charles the Second, Father of His Country, the

belle & Reguliere. Son Clocher est parfaitement beau & a au haut un Carillon qui est un des Meilleurs de **Londres**. En y entrant par la Grande Ruë, on voit à Chaque coté de la porte dans une Niche, la Statuë de Charles I. & de Charles II. Quand vous etes entré dans la Bourse vous appercevez d'abord la Statuë Pedestré de Charles II. en Marbre avec une Inscription Latin que voicy.

Carolo Secundo, Cæsari Britannico, Patriæ Patri, Regum Optimo, Clementissimo, Augustissimo, Generis Humani Deliciis, Utriusque Fortunæ Victori, Pacis Europæ Arbitro, Maris Domino & Vindici.

Societas Mercatorum Adventur. Angliæ, quæ per CCCC jam Annos Regia Benignitate floret, Fidei intemeratæ, & Gratitudinis Æternæ, hoc Testimonium venerabundæ posuit, Anno Salutis 1684.

the beſt of Kings, moſt Clement, moſt Auguſt, the Delight of Mankind, Arbitrator of the Peace of *Europe*, Lord and Avenger of the Seas.

The Society of *Engliſh* Merchant - Adventurers, which for theſe 400 Years has flouriſh'd under Royal Favour.

On the Weſt-ſide of the *Exchange* under the Piazzas, is the Statue of Sir *Thomas Greſham*, who was one of the firſt Merchants of *London* that ſent Ships to the *Eaſt-Indies*, which having brought him immenſe Riches, he built the firſt *Exchange*: but it was burnt at the Fire of *London*. He has a Letter in his Hand; this is the Reaſon of it, and which deſerves to be incerted here. This Knight having exhauſted himſelf to fit out his Ships, which were out a long Time before they returned, and being preſſed by his Creditors, he applyed himſelf to his Brother, intreating him to lend him a Sum

Au Coin Occidental de la Bourſe & ſous les Arcades ſe void la Statuë du Chevalier Greſham, *qui a eté un des premiers Marchands de* Londres *des qui envoya Vaiſſeaux aux* Indes-Orientales, *les quels lui en ayant rapporté des Richeſſes immenſes il fit batir la premiere* Bourſe: *mais elle fut brulée à l'Incendie de* Londres. *Il a une Lettre a la Main, en Voici la Raiſon, qui merite bien d'etre rapportée icy. Ce Chevalier s'etant epuiſe pour Equiper ſes Vaiſſeaux qui furent longtems a revenir, & le trouvant preſſé par ſes Creanciers il s'adreſſa au Chevalier ſon frere le priant de lui pretter une ſomme pour*

a Sum of Money to satisfy them; his Brother refused him, adding, he did not know him. Hereupon he met all his Creditors and begged of them to give him two Months Time more, which they did; and that Time was elapſed all but three or four Days, when a Sailor came to the *Exchange* and inquir'd, whether Sir *Thomas Greſham* was there? he found him out and deliver'd that Letter to him, which acquainted him that two of his Ships were arrived from the *Eaſt-Indies*, and delivering a Box-Caſe to him in which were ſeveral Diamonds and Pearls of great Value; *Sir* (ſaid he) *theſe are but a Sample of the Immenſe Riches your Ships have brought you.* He thereby became indeed one of the Richeſt Merchants in the Univerſe. His Relations and his own Brother, as we ſaid before, had forſaken him in his Neceſſity, he would never own afterwards, and he lay'd out all

pour les ſatisfaire: Son frere lui dit qu'il ne le connoiſſoit point. Sur ce refus il aſſembla ſes Creanciers & les pria de lui accorder deux mois de tems; ce qu'ils firent; & il ne s'en falloit que quatre Jours, lors qu'un Marinier vint ſur la Bourſe & demanda ſi le Chevalier Thomas Greſham y etoit? il le trouva & lui remit cette Lettre qui lui annonçoit l'Arrivée de deux de ſes Vaiſſeaux des Indes, & en lui remettant un Bœtier avec pluſieurs Diamands & Perles de grand Prix; Monſieur dit il ceci n'eſt qu'un Echantillon dés Richeſſes Immenſes que vous recevrez par vos Vaiſſeaux. Elles le rendirent effectivement un des plus Riches Marchands de l'Univers. Ses Parens & ſon Frere même comme nous l'avons dit, l'avoient abandonné dans ſa Neceſſité, il ne les voulut jamais reconnoitre; & il employa tous ſes Biens a batir des Edifices Publics, dont la premiere Bourſe en etoit un, le Collge de Gre-
ſham,

BIBLIOTHÈQUE DE L'ARSENAL

all his Wealth in Building publick Edifices, of which the first *Exchange* was one, *Gresham*-College (which he Endowed with considerable Revenues, founding therein six Professorships, *viz.* one of Divinity, of Law, of Physick, of Philosophy, of Astronomy, and one of Musick, to give publick Lessons on the Sciences for ever) was another of his Foundations, as well as several Hospitals. He made also considerable Donations to many Societies and Families. The Grashopper, that is the Weather Cock on the Steeple of the *Royal-Exchange*, is there, because it was the Crest of that Illustrious Benefactor's Coat of Arms. Here is a Passage that will let you into his Character. Sir *Thomas* being at Court when the *Spanish* Embassador extoll'd the great Riches of the King his Master, and of the Grandees of his Kingdom, to the famous Queen *Elizabeth*, Sir *Thomas* told him, that the Queen had Subjects who at one Meal expended

sham, qu'il dota de Revenus Considerables, etablissant un Professeur en Theologie, en Droit, en Medecine, en Philosophie, en Astronomie, & un en Musique, pour donner des Leçons Publiques a Perpetuité, en etoit un autre, aussi bien que plusieurs Hopitaux. Et fit des Donations Considerables a une Infinité de Societés, & de Familles. La Sauterelle qui sert de Girouette au Clocher de la Bourse, y est parce que cétoit le Cimier des Armes de cet Illustre Bienfaiteur. Voici encore un trait qui fera connoitre son Charactere. Le Chevalier etant a la Cour un Jour que l'Ambassadeur d'Espagne vantoit a la fameuse Reine Elizabeth, les grandes Richesses du Roy son Maitre & des Grands de son Royaume, le Chevalier lui dit que la Reine avoit des sujets, qui dans un seul repas depensoient valeur du Revenu d'un Jour non seulement de son Roy, mais aussi de tous

pended not only as much as the Revenues of his King, but also of all his Grandees amounted to for one Day, and would lay he'd prove it when he pleas'd; they laid a considerable Sum; the Ambassador came one Day at unawares to Sir *Thomas's*, and Din'd with him, finding only an Ordinary Meal. *Well*, sai'd he, *Sir you have Lost!* *Not at all*, said Sir *Thomas*, *your self shall be Judge of it.* At the same Time he pulled a Box out of his Pocket, and takes one of the largest and finest *Eastern* Pearls out of it, he Grinds it, and drank the Powder of it in a Glass of Wine! *My Lord Ambassador*, said he, *you know I have often refused 150,000 Pounds for it*, have I Lost or Won? *I yield the Wager Lost*, said the Ambassador, *and I don't think there are four Subjects in the World that would do as much for the Honour of their Sovereign.* But let us return to our Subject: Round the Change, in the

tous ses Grands! & qu'il gageoit de le lui prouver quand il voudroit; ils parièrent une Somme Considerable; l'Ambassadeur vint un jour surprendre ce Chevalier, & dina avec lui, ne trouvant qu'un Repas assez simple; he bien, dit il, vous avez perdu! Point du tout, *dit le Chavalier*, & vous même me en serez le Juge. *En meme tems il tire de sa poche un Boitier et en prend une des plus grosses & des plus belles Perles de l'Orient, il la broye et en avalle la Poudre dans un Verre de Vin.* Mr. L'Ambassadeur (*dit il*) vous sçavez que que j'en ai *souvent refusez* 150,000 Livres Sterlin, ay je Perdu ou Gagné? *Je vous ce de la Gageure, dit l'Ambassadeur, & je ne crois pas que l'on trouve quatre sujets dans le Monde, qui en voulussent faire autant pour l'Honneur de leur Souverain. Mais revenons a notre Sujet: tout a l'Entout de la Bourse dans la Cour & au dessus des Arcades vous voyez dans*

the Court and above the Piazza's you see in Niches the Statues of K. *Edward* III. *Henry* V. *Edward* IV. *Edward* V. *Henry* VII. *Henry* VIII *Edward* VI. *Mary* I. *Elizabeth*, *James* I. *Charles* I. *Charles* II. *James* II. *William* III. & *Mary* II. and of King *George*.

Above in the said *Exchange* there are near 200 Mercers, Milliners, and Toy-Shops, and other Shops. And under it there are spacious Vaults full of Pepper, &c. round the whole, on the outsides are Shops of all sorts, which is the Reason that this Building, though so small, brings in near 4000 *l. per Annum.* In short, it may be affirmed, there is no *Exchange* in the Universe so fine as this, and that it is justly distinguish'd from them, by the Title of *Royal-Exchange.* The Merchants meet there about their Business and Trade, from two in the Afternoon to near four. It is also before this *Exchange* that the Proclamations of War and Peace are made; they

dans des Niches les Ssatuës des Rois *Edward* III. Henry V. Edward IV. Edward V. Henri VII. Henri VIII. Edward VI. Marie I. Elizabeth, Jaques I. Charles I. Charles II. Jaques II. Guillaume III. & Marie II. & du Roi George.

Au haut de la dite Bourse *il y a environ* 200 Boutiques de Quincaliers, Merciers, Lingeres, &c. & au dessous il y a de spacieuses voutes pleines de Poivre, &c. tout a l'entour il y a en dehors des Boutiques de toutes Sortes de Marchandises, ce qui fait que ce Batiment quoique si Petit rapporte près de 4000 Liv. Ster. par An. En fin l'on peut dire qu'il n'y a point de Bourse en l'Univers qui soit si belle que celle-ce, & que c'est avec droit, qu'elle porte le Titre de Bourse-Royale. Les Marchands s'y Assemblent pour traiter des Affaires de leur Negoce depuis deux heures après Midy jusqu'a prés de quatre Heures. C'est aussi devant cette Bourse que se font les Proclamations de Guerre

they are first Proclaimed at St. *James's*, secondly at *Charing-Cross*, thirdly at *Temple-Bar*, fourthly at the *Royal-Exchange*, and fifthly at the Tower of *London*. It is also before this *Exchange* that Persons are put in the Pillory after they have been exposed therein at *Charing-Cross*, and *Temple-Bar*. From hence you may go to see the *General Post-Office*; and the Church adjoining thereto, which are two Magnificent Buildings. And after that, if it be about ten in the Morning, or three in the Afternoon, you may view the Church of St. *Peter's Cornhill*, wherein there is an Inscription that affirms it was the first Metropolitan Church in *England*, and therefore it has a Key for its Weathercock.

Thence you may go to *Leaden-Hall Market*, it is the largest and best of all the Markets in *London*, and they say there is as much Meat sold here in a Week, as they sell in a whole Month in *Paris*. Near

Guerre & de Paix, dont les Processions commencent à faire la premiere Proclamation à St. James, la seconde à Charing-Cross, la troisiéme à Temple-Bar, la quatrieme à la Bourse, & la quinquieme a la Tour de Londres. C'est aussi devant cette Bourse qu'on expose les Criminels au Carquan; apres qu'on les y a auparavant exposé à Charing-Cross & a Temple-Bar. De là vous pourrez aller voir le Bureau de la Grande Poste, & la nouvelle Eglise qui y joint, & qui sont deux magnifiques Edifices. Et ensuite si c'est à dix heures du Matin, ou à trois apres Midy, vous irez voir l'Eglise de St. Pierre au Coin de Cornhil, dans laquelle il y a une Inscription qui marque qu'elle a eté la premiere Eglise Metropolitaine d'Angleterre; & c'est pourquoi elle a la Clef pour sa Girouette.

De là vous vous ferez mener a Leadenhal Market c'est le plus grand & le meilleur de tous les Marchez de Londres & on dit qu'on y vend autant de viande en une semaine qu'il s'en vend en un Mois dans tout Paris. Proche

Near this Place is the East-India House; the Goods in the Warehouses belonging to it, just before the Sale, are well worth seeing. From hence you go to

Proche de là est la Maison des Indes, les Magazines, & les Marchandises sont dignes de votre curiosité, sur tout quand elles sont disposés pour les Ventes. De là vous vous ferez conduire au

The Monument.

Le Monument.

IT is a Magnificent Column, which was Erected in perpetual Memory of the dreadful Fire of *London*, and it is behind this Column to the East that the Fire began at a Baker's call'd *Fariners*. Directly over against the entry into the said Street, behind the *Monument* above the Door of the said House, you see an *English* Inscription graved on Marble, and is thus,

Here by the Permission of Heaven, Hell broke loose against this Protestant City, by the Malice of the Hearts of the Cruel Papists, and by the Hand of their Agent Hubert, who upon the Ruins of this Place, confess'd and declared the Fact, for which he was hang'd;
viz.

CE'st une Colomne Magnifique, qui a été erigée en Memoire perpetuelle du terrible Incendie de Londres, & c'est derriere cette Colomne que le Feu commença dans la Maison d'un Boulenger nommée Fariners; vis a vis de l'entrées dans la Rue qui est derriere le Monument au dessus de la Porte de cette Maison on lit une Inscription en Anglois gravée en Marbre, dont voici la traduction:

C'est icy que par la Permission du Ciel, l'Enfer se déchaina contre cette Ville Protestante par la Malignité des Coeurs des cruels Papistes, & par la main de leur Agent Hubert; qui confess. & declara sur les ruines de ce Lieu, le Fait pour lequel il fut pendu; sçavoir,
qu'icy

viz. that in this Place began that terrible Fire, which is Described and Perpetuated on the Neighbouring Pillar, Erected Anno Dom. 1671. *in the Mayoralty of Sir R. Forde.*

Round the first Plint or Edge of this Pillar, you have the following Inscription, which was put thereon by Order of the said Lord Mayor and Aldermen.

This Pillar was Erected in perpetual Memory of the Terrible - - - - - - - of this Protestant City, contrived and - - - - - - - - by the Perfidiousneß and Malice of the Papists in the beginning of Septemb. 1666. *in order to execute the execrable Plot made to extirpate the Protestant Religion and the - - - - - -* English *Liberty, and to introduce Popery and Slavery.*

On the face towards the Street there is a *Latin* Inscription, the Translation of which is as follows.

qu'icy commença ce terrible Feu, qui est décrit & perpetué sur la Collomne voisine, erigée Anno Dom. 1671. dans le Majorat du Chevalier R. Forde.

Tout à l'entour du premier Cordon de cette Collomne on voit l'Inscription suivante qui y a eté mise par Ordre du susdit Lord Maire & des Echevins.

Ce Pillier a eté erigé en Memoire Perpetuelle de du Terrible Incendie de cette Ville Protestante, tramée & executée par la perfidie & la Malice des Papistes au commencement de *September* 1666. afin de pouvoir executer l'execrable Complot fait pour extirper la Religion Protestante & l'ancienne Liberté *Angloise,* & pour introduire le Papisme & l'Esclavage.

Sur la face du Coté de la Rue il y a une Inscription Latin dont voicy la Traduction.

In the Year of our Lord 1666, on the second day of September there arose within 202 Foot from hence (which is exactly the heighth of this Column) a Conflagration, towards Midnight, which being encreas'd by the Wind, spread far and wide through all the Places of this very Populous City, and destroy'd with incredible Rapidity and Noise, 84 Churches, Gates, Courts, Publick Buildings, Halls, Schools, several large Libraries, 400 Streets, and above 13200 Houses. Of the 26 Wards of the City 15 were entirely ruined to the very Foundations, and 8 others were much damaged. The Ruins of the City extended to 436 Acres, from this Pillar along the Shore to the West, as far as the Temple Chapel, and, to the North-East as far as the Walls above Fleet-ditch; to the great Misfortune and Ruin of the Inhabitants, and loss of the Lives of the Innocent; so that it seem'd to be the Conflagration which was to reduce the Universe to Ashes.

L'In-

L'An de Grace 1666 le seconde de *Septembre*, il s'eleva a 202 Pieds d'icy (ce qui est justement la hauteur de cette Colomne) un Incendie vers la Minuit, laquelle etant augmentée par le vent s'etendit au long & au large par tous les endroits de cette Ville si Peuplée, & detruisit avec une impetuosité & un bruit incroyable 84 Eglises, Portes, Cours, Edifices Publics, Halles, Echoles, plusieurs Grandes Bibliotheques, 400 Rües, & plus de 13200 Maisons. Des 26 Quartiers de la Ville, 15 furent entirement ruinés jusqu'-aux fondemens & 8 autres furent fort endommagés. Les Ruines de la Ville s'etendoient a 436 Arpens depuis cette Colomne le long du Rivage a l'occident jusqu'a l'Eglise du Temple, & au Nord Est, jusqu'a la Porte sur les Murailles au haut de *Fleetditth*; au grand Malheur & a la Ruins des habitans, & de la vie des Innocens, de sorte qu'il sembloit que c'etoit l'embrasement qui devoit deduire l'Univers en Cendres.

The

The Burning was so swift and sudden, that those who a little before had seen a flourishing City, could see no remains of it.

The third Day, when all human Means and Assistance were exhausted, it pleased God, contrary to all Expectation, to put a stop to the Fire and extinguish it.

On the face towards the Back-Street.

Charles *the Second,* Son of Charles *the Martyr,* King *of* Great Britain, France *and* Ireland, *Defender of the* Faith, *a most* Clement Prince, *who having* Compassion *of the* Loss *occasion'd by* Fire, *to the greatest Part of the Inhabitants of this City (the* Ruins *of which were yet smoaking) and which before that was his greatest* Glory, *was pleased to provide for it; he remitted their* Taxes, *and recommended them to the Parliament, who thereupon Ordered that the* Publick Buildings *should be rebuilt in a better Structure than they*

L'Incendie fut si rapide & soudaine qu'entres peu de tems on avoit vu une Ville florissante & il n'en restoit aucunes Traces.

Le troisieme Jour lors que tous les Remedes & les Assistances humaines etoient epüisez, il plut au Ciel, contre toute croyance d'arreter le Feu & de l'eteindre.

Sur la Face du Coté de la Ruë de derriere.

Charles Second Fils de *Charles* le Martyr Roi de la *Grande Bretagne,* de *France,* & d'Irlande Defenseur de la Foy, Prince tres Clement, ayant eu Compassion de la perte causée par l'incendie a la plus grande partie des Habitans & a cette Ville, (dont le Ruïnes etoient encore fumante) & qui etoit auparavant sa plus grande Gloire, voulut bien y pourvoir; il leur remit les Taxes & les recommende auParlement, qui la dessus ordonna que les Batimens Publics seroient rebati d'une meilleure Structure qu'ils n'e-

they   toient

they were before, from the Moneys arising from the Duty upon Coals, viz. the Churches and the Cathedral of St. Paul's, were to be rebuilt from the Foundations with all possible Magnificence: That they should rebuild the Bridges, Gates and Prisons; that the Common-Shores should be cleansed, that the Descents should be levelled, that the narrow Streets or Lanes, Highways and Markets, should be made wider; that no House should be built without a Separation-Wall between each; that they must be all of the same heighth forwards, and of polish'd Free-Stones or Bricks; and lastly, that none should be above Seven Years in rebuilding his House. Adding also an annual Fast-Day for a perpetual Memorial thereof to Posterity.

H. C. P. C.

People were earnest on all Parts, so that there was reason to doubt whether London recover'd itself.

toient auparavant, des Deniers Publics provenant de l'Impôt sur le Charbon de Terre la Houille, scavoir, les Eglises & la Cathedrale de St. Paul, seroient rebaties dès les fondemens avec toute la Magnificence possible; que l'on rebatiroit les Ponts, Ports & Prisons, que les Egouts seroient nettoyés, que les descentes seroient aplanies, que l'on elargiroit les Rues etroites les Chemins & les Marchez. Que l'on ne batiroit point de Maison sans une Muraille de separation entredeux, qu'elles seroient toutes de meme hauteur sur le Devant & de Pierre de Taille Polies ou de Briques; enfin que Personne ne seroit plus de sept Ans à rebatir sa Maison. Ajoutant un jour de Jeune annuel pour Memorial perpetuel a la Posterité.

H. C. P. C.

On s'empressa de tous cotés de sorte, qu'il y avoit Lieu de douter si Londres s'etoit relevé le plus.

Trois

Three Years compleated what it was thought would have been the Work of an Age, a Century.

Began under the Mayoralty of Richard Forde, *Mayor of* London, *A. D. 1671. and very far advanced under*

Georgius Waterman
Roberto Hanfon.
Gulielm. Hooker.
Roberto Viner.
Jofeph. Shelden,

Compleated in the Mayoralty of Thomas Davies. *Anno. Dom.* MDCLXXI.

You give Two Pence to go up to the top of this Pillar, where you have a very fine Profpect of the City, the River of *Thames,* and the Country. When you are come down from this Pillar, you may, as you go down the fame Street, obferve a Church on which there is a fine Dial, the Clock of which (they fay) can go a hundred Years without being wound up. And as foon as you are beyond this Church you come upon

London

Trois Ans acheva ce qu'on avoit cru devoir etre l'Ouvrage d'un Siecle.

Commencé fous le Majorat de *Richard Forde,* Maire de *London,* A. D. 1671. poufté fort haut fous

Georgius Waterman.
Roberto Hanfon.
Guliel. Hooker.
Roberto Viner.
Jofeph Sheldon

Perfectioné ou fini fous Le Majorat de *Thoma Davies. An. Dom.* MDCLXXI.

On donne deux Sous pour monter au haut de cette Collomne, que vous aurez confiderez la belle Vuë qu'on y a de la Ville, de la Riviere Thames, & de la Campagne. Apres que vous en ferez defcendu vous pourez en defcendant la meme Ruë remarquer une Eglife ou il y a un beau Quadran, & dont l'horloge peut aller (a ce qu'on dit,) cent Ans fans la monter. Et dès que vous le aurez paffée vous vous trouverez fur le

E 4

Pont

London-Bridge,

UPon which there are three Views upon the River, the firſt is the Drawbridge, on the South Eaſt of which there was formerly a Chapel, on the third is the Houſe called the *Nonſuch*, being all made of Wood, and without any Iron or Nails. This Bridge has 19 Arches is 800 Foot long, 30 broad and 60 Foot high: At the end of it is one of the Gates of the City. When you have ſeen it all, go and ſee the Water-Mill that furniſhes Water to a great Part of the City. Afterwards, you may, if you pleaſe, ſee *Fiſhmongers-Hall*, which is hard by it, and is a ſumptuous Building. Thence going back to the Church aforeſaid at the foot of the Bridge, turning to the Right towards the Eaſt, you come to

Pont le Londres,

SUr lequel il y a trois Vuës ſur la Riviere la premiere eſt le Pont Levis à l'Orient duquel il y avoit autrefois une Chapelle, & a la troiſieme eſt la Maiſon dite ſans Pareille, etant toute faite de Bois & ſans aucuns Cloux, ni Ferrements. Ce Pont a dix neuf Arches, 800 Pieds de long, 30 de large, & 60 de hauteur: Aubout de ce Pont eſt une des Portes de la Ville. Quand vous l'aurez vu d'un bout a l'autre, voyez le Moulin qui fournit d'eau a une grande Partie de la Ville. Et enſuite vous verrez, ſi vous la ſouhaité, l'Hotel de la Compagnie des Poiſſoniers, qui en eſt tout proche & qui eſt un tres bel Edifice. De la remontez vers l'Egliſe ſuſdite au bas du Pont & en Montant a Droite vers l'Orient, vous viendrez a

Billingsgate,

Billingsgate.

WHere you have a very good Fish-Market, and the beft and frefheft Oyfters in *London*, and in all the Taverns thereabouts the beft Canary in *England* to help you to digeft them. Going thence to the River-fide Eaftward you come to the

Cuftom-Houfe,

WHere you will be furprifed to fee the vaft quantity of Merchandifes and Goods of all forts, that are loaded and unloaded there conftantly, and with which the Wharfs are fo overfilled that one can fcarce pafs there. Obferve the Frontifpiece of the Cuftom-Houfe which is lately rebuilt, having been burnt not long fince with about 30 Houfes and Warehoufes in the Neighbourhood. Go afterwards

Billingsgate.

OU l'on trouve une fort bonne Poiffonnerie & les Meilleures & les plus Fraiches Huitres de Londres, & dans toutes les Tavernes des environs le meilleur Vin d'Efpagne qu'il y ait en Angleterre pour en facilliter de Digeftion. Defcendant enfuite vers le bord de la Riviere à l'Orient vous venez à la

Douane,

OU vous ferez furpris de voir la grande quantité de Marchandifes de toutes fortes qui s'y chargent & dechargent continuellement, & dont la Plage eft fi remplie qu'on de la Peine y paffer. Remarqué le Frontifpice de la Douane qui eft depuis peu rebati, ayant eté brulé il y a quelque tems avec une trentaine de Maifons & Magafins des Environs. Montez enfuite dans la Douane & obfervez en les Tapifferies, entrez y par un bout & fortez

terwards into the Custom House and see the Hangings that are there, you go in at one end and come out at the other. Thence you come to the

Tower of London.

THis Tower was built by *William the Conqueror*, and enlarged by several of his Successors. It was here the Kings went formerly to dwell some Days at the beginning of their Reigns; and this Abode or Retirement here was call'd their taking Possession of the Kingdom. This Fortress was also a place of secure Retreat for Kings in the Civil Wars or Insurrections of the Subjects. And now it is the Prison of Noble Criminals of State. The Records and the Regal Ornaments are kept here. It is the great Arsenal of the Kingdom, and herein is also the Great Mint of the Kingdom, where almost all the Gold, Silver, and Copper Coin in the Realm, is struck.

It

sortez en par l'autre. De là vous venez à la

Tour de *Londres.*

CEtte *Tour a été Batie par* Guillaume *le* Conquerant, *& agrandie par plusieurs de ses Successeurs. C'étoit là que les Rois alloient autrefois demeurer quelques jours au commencement de leur Regnes, & cette demeure ou retraite etoit regardée comme la prise de Possession du Gouvernement. Cette Fortresse etoit aussi une Retraite pour les Rois dans les Guerres Civiles ou Soulevemens des Peuple. A present c'est la Prison des Seigneurs & Gentilshommes Criminels d'Etats. C'est là que l'on garde les Archives & les Ornemens de la Regale. C'est le Grand Arsenal du Royaume, & c'est aussi là que l'on frappe toute la Monnoye d'Or, & presque toute celle d'Argent & de Cuivre du Royaume. Elle*

en

It is governed by a Constable, who commonly is a Peer of the Realm, the Duke of *Bolton* is the present Constable thereof, he has a Deputy Governor under him, and here is a Garrison besides the Guards, called *Warders of the Tower.*

When you go therein through the Great Gate, you see on your Right-hand the Figure of a Lion painted over the Door, knock at that Door and they will shew you some Lions, Panthers, Tygers, Eagles, Vultures, an Ostrich, and other rare Beasts and Birds; You must pay Three-pence a-piece to see them.

Thence you'll go further into the *Tower,* and you must leave your Sword with the Warders of the Tower; one of them will wait on you to shew you all the Curiosities thereof.

They bring you first to see the Arsenal, where they carefully keep (1.) All the Arms that were taken on the Fleet, arrogantly called the *Invincible*

est gouvernée par un Connetable qui est ordinairement Pair du Royaume, c'est le Duc de Bolton qui l'est à present, il a un Sous Gouverneur sous lui, & il y a une Garrison, outre les Gardes qu'on appelle Warders of the Tower.

En y entrant par la Grand Porte vous voyez a Droite la Figure d'un Lion, peinte au dessus d'une Porte, frappez y & on vous fera voir des Lions, des Pantheres, Tigres, Aigles, Vautours, Ostriche, & plusieurs autres Betes & Oiseaux Rares; vous donnez trois Sols par tete pour les voir.

De là vous entrez plus avant dans la Tour, & il faut que vous laissiez votre Epée aux Gardes de la Tour, l'un des quels vous accompagnera pour vous en faire voir toutes les Curiosités.

On vous mene premierement voir un Arsenal, où l'on garde soigneusement (1.) Toutes les Armes qui furent prises sur la Flotte arrogamment appellée *Invin-*

ble *Armado*, by *Philip* the Second of *Spain*, and which, as before said, was destroy'd in 1588, by the *English* under Q. *Elizabeth*, by the *Dutch*, and by the Storms. (2.) Some Cannon and Arms taken from the Duke of *Monmouth*. (3.) The Ax wherewith was cut off the Head of *Anne* of *Boulogne*, Mother to Queen *Elizabeth*. (4.) A wooden Cannon with this Inscription, *Marte quid opus est, cui Minerva non deest.* Which was put thereon as a Memorial that the *English* formerly took a Town in *France*, which they frighten'd to a Surrender by wooden Guns. You pay here Two Pence each.

Near this Place is another Arsenal, where they will shew you several Kings on Horseback with their Armour, and also a vast quantity of Arms, Breast and Head-Pieces, &c.

Then you will go to see the Regalia, and you must each pay Half a Crown. They shew you, 1. The

Invincible Armado, par Philip Second d'Espagne, & qui fut, comme nous l'avons dit, détruite en 1588, par les Anglois sous la Reine Elisabeth, par les Hollandois, & par la Tempête. (2.) *Quelques Cannons & Armes pris sur le Duc de Monmouth.* (3.) *La Hache avec laquelle on trancha la Tête à Anne de Boulogne Mere de la Reine Elizabeth.* (4.) *Un Cannon de Bois avec cette Inscription,* Marte quid opus est, cui Minerva non deest, *Ce qui y a été mis en Memoire de ce que les Anglois prirent autrefois une Ville en France en l'intimidant par des Cannons de Bois. Vous donnez là Chacun deux Sous ou plus.*

Proche de là il y a un autre Arsenal où on vous montrera plusieurs Rois à Cheval dans leurs Cuirasses, & quantité d'Armes, de Cuirasses, &c.

Ensuite vous irés voir le lieu où l'on garde la Regale & vous y donnerez chacun 30 Sous. On vous montrera d'a-bord

1. The Crown of State which the King wears when he goes to the Parliament.

2. The Crown of St. *Edward* the Confessor.

3. The Staff of that Holy King.

4. The Crown which the Queens wear when they go to *Westminster* to be Crowned.

5. The Crown with which the Queens are Crown'd.

6. The Crown of State for the Queen.

7. The Globe which the King carries in his Left-hand.

8. The Scepter which he holds in his Right-hand.

9. The Scepter of Peace having a Dove on the top, and which is carried in Ceremony before the King at his Coronation.

10. The Queens Globe.

11. The Queens Scepter

12. The Scepter of Peace that is carri'd before her at her Coronation.

13. A Scepter of Ivory that was given to King *James* the 2d's Queen.

14. A

1. La Couronne d'etat que le Roy porte quand il est au Parlement.

2. La Couronne de St. Edouard *le Confesseur*.

3. La Croß de ce Saint Roy.

4. La Couronne que les Reines portent lors qu'elles vont à Westminster pour être Couronnés.

5. La Couronne avec laquelle les Reines sont Couronnées.

6. La Couronne d'Etat pour la Reine.

7. Le Globe que le Roy porte en sa Main-Gauche.

8. Le Sceptre qu'il tient de la Main Droite.

9. Le Sceptre de Paix ayant au haut une Colombe & qui se porte en Ceremonie devant le Roy à son Couronnement.

10. Le Globe de la Reine.

11. Le Sceptre de la Reine.

12. Le Sceptre de Paix qui se porte devant elle à son Couronnement.

13. Un Sceptre d'Yvoire qui fut presenté à la Reine Epouse de Jaques 2d.

14. Un

13. A Golden Eagle wherein the Oyl is put wherewith the Kings are Anointed with; and a Golden Spoon to take it out of the same.

15. Two Golden Spurs and two Bracelets which the Kings and Queens wear the Day they are Crown'd.

16, 17, and 18. The Sword without a Point, called the Sword of Mercy, the Sword of State, and the Sword with a Point; which are Symbols of the Power, Clemency and Justice of Kings; and which are carried in Ceremony before the Kings the Day they are Crown'd.

19. A very fine Salt-Seller of double Gilt Silver, made after the Shape and Model of the square Tower in the middle of the Tower of *London*, the Turrets whereof are put upon the King's Table the Day he is Crown'd.

20. A Christening Font for the Children of the Royal Family, with two Pots all of Silver double Gilt, which are us'd to pour

14. *Un Aigle d' Or où on renferme l' Huile dont on oint & sacre les Rois, & une Cueillere d' Or, pour l' entirer.*

15. *Deux Eperons d' Or, & deux Bracelets que les Rois & les Reines portent le Jour de leurs Couronne-mens.*

16, 17, & 18. *Un Glaive ou Epée sans Pointe, appellé l' Epée de Mercy, l' Epée d' Etat, & l' Epée a Pointes; Symboles de la Puissance, de la Clemence, & de la Justice des Rois, & qui se portent en Ceremonie devant le Rois les Jours de leurs Couronne-ment.*

19. *Une tres belle Saliere de Vermeil doré faite à l'Imitation de la Tour quarrée qui est au Millieu de la Tour de* Londres, *& dont les quatres Tourettes se mettent sur la Table du Roy le Jour de son Couronnement.*

20. *Un Font de Batême pour les Enfans de la Maison Royale, avec deux Pots aussi de vermeil Doré, dont on se pour verser l' Eau, &*

pour the Water, and a Silver Fountain finely wrought to hold the Water.

All these Jewels are of Silver double Gilt, and the Work is so exquisitely fine, the Precious Stones that enrich them are so large, and in such great Numbers, that it is impossible to guess the Value of them or to forbear to admire them.

When you are come out of this Place you go directly to another great Arsnal, where they'll shew you a Train of Artillery, and several Cannon and Mortars of a new Invention: Here is, among the rest, a very fine Cannon and extraordinary large, which they call *Queen Elizabeth's Pocket Pistol:* And a Bell in which they put a Man in when they let him down to the Bottom of the Sea, to fasten to a Rope what they have a mind to take up from thence. You pay here Two-Pence each.

And from thence you go to the Upper Arsenal, which is one of the finest

in

Et une Fountaine d'Argent, tres bien travaillée.

Tous ces Bijoux sont de Vermeil Doré, & le travail en est si exquis, les Pierres Precieuses qui les enrichissent sont si grosses, si belles, & en si grand Nombre, qu'il est impossible de les Evalluer & de se lasser de les admirer.

Etant sortis de cet endroit vous allez directement à un autre Arsenal où on vous montrera un Train d'Artillerie, & plusieurs Cannons & Mortiers d'une nouvelle Invention. Il y a là un Cannon tres beau & d'un Calibre extraordinaire qu'on appelle, Le Pistolet de Poche de la Reine Elizabeth : Et une Clocke dans la quelle on renferme un Homme lors qu'on veut le descendre au fond de la Mer pour y attacher ce qu'on a dessein d'en retirer. On paye là deux Sols chacun.

Et de là vous montez, a l'Arsenal Superieur, qui est l'un des plus beaux de l'Eu-

in *Europe*, both for the nice Order the Arms are plac'd in, as for the great Quantity of them. You pay here alſo Two-Pence each.

Thoſe who will ſee the Mint may go there, and they muſt give the Workmen ſomething to drink.

Going out of the *Tower* near the Guard on the Eaſt, you will ſee a Draw-Bridge and a Gate, it is call'd the *Traitor's-Bridge* and *Gate*. The State Criminals paſs this Way when they are going to be executed. Here you will diſcharge the Warder that attended you, and give him a Shilling or two for his Pains.

When you have carefully examined all theſe Things, as well as the Chapel, the Batteries and other Places and Streets in the *Tower*, the fine Proſpect of the Ships on the *Thames*, &c. you may go to *Tower-Hill*, in order to conſider it all round on the outſide. As you go from the Great Gate you come to the Navy-Office, which is not extraor-

l'Europe, tant par le bel Arrangement, que pour la Quantité de belles Armes qu'on y tient en tres bon Etat. On donne icy auſſi deux Sous chacun.

Ceux qui voudront voir battre la Monoye pourront y aller & donneront quelque choſe à boire aux Monnoyeurs.

En ſortant de la Tour à l'Orient vous verrez une Porte avec un Pont-Levis on l'appelle le Pont & la Porte des Traitres: C'eſt par où les Criminels d'Etat paſſent pour aller à la Mort. Là vous congedierez votre Garde & lui donnerez un Chelin ou deux pour ſa Peine.

Quand vous aurez Examinés curieuſement toutes ces Choſes, auſſi bien que la Chapelle, les Bateries & les autres endroits & Rues de la Tour, la belle Vuë des Vaiſſeaux ſur la Thamiſes, &c. vous monterez ſur la Hauteur qu'on appelle Tower-Hill, laquelle environne toute la Tour, afin de la Conſiderer extérieurement. Il y a en montant de la grande Porte l'Office de la Marine, qui

traordinary. On the East of that Hill is also the Victualling-Office. Get your self to be brought to the *Minories*, and going up that Street you see before you the fine Steeple of St. *Dunstan's* Church; then you come to *Aldgate*, and going up *Hounsditch* you come to *Bishopsgate-street*. Between these two last Gates is *Dukes-Place*, where most of the *Jews* dwell; you may on a *Saturday* go and see their Synagogue, which is very fine, but the Streets of their resort are very dirty and disagreeable. Going out of the Gate you enter on the left into a narrow Street that brings you to *Moorfields*, thus called from Mr. *Moor* who gave those Fields to the Washer-women of *London*, to hang out and dry their Linnen there. At the bottom of the lower of these Fields is the Mad-House called *Bedlam*, it is a very magnificent Building and very regular, wherein they confine Mad Men and Women

qu'en a rien d'extraordinaire. A l'Orient de cette hauteur est l'Office de l'Avitaillement des vaisseaux du Roy. Faites vous conduire vers les Minories, & en montant cette Ruë vous voyez le beau Clocher de l'Eglise de St. Dunstan; & vous viendrez a Aldgate, puis suivant la Ruë de Hounsditch vous venez dans la Ruë de Bishopsgate ou Porte l'Eveque. Entre ces deux Portes est le Quartier des Juifs où vous pourez le Samedy aller voir leur Synagogue qui est tres belle, mais les Ruës de leur quartiers sont tres mal propres & desagreables. En sortant hors de la Porte a Gauche vous entrez dans une petit Ruë qui vous mene a Moorfields, ainsi nommé du Sieur Moor qui donne ces Prez aux Blanchisseuses de Londres, pour y etendre & secher leur Linge. Au midy & au bas de ces Prez est la Maison des Foux qu'on appelle Bedlam, c'est un magnifique Edifice, & fort regulier, où l'on remfermes les Foux & les Lunatiques. Et a Coté de ce Batiment a

men and the Lunaticks. And next to this Building on the East there is a House to receive Incurables; go in there and observe those afflicted Persons, their different State will move you, and you will find merry Objects there; and at the same time you will have reason to thank God for the favour he has done you to keep you from the sad Condition these unfortunate Objects are reduced to! You must each pay a Peny when you go out.

The *French* Pest-House is a little above these Fields, it is both their Hospital and Mad-house. You may go there if you please, and go at the same time to the fine Hospital at *Hoxton*, which is near it, called *Aske's Hospital*, founded to lodge and maintain 20 poor Men who are Free of the Haberdashers Company.

This is a magnificent Foundation to be made by a private Person, but it is suppos'd he did it only

L'Orient il y aura une Maison pour recevoir ceux dont le Delire est Incurable; entrez y, & observez les Personnes Affligées qui y sont renfermés, leurs differens Etats vous toucheront, & vous y trouverez de quoy vous divertir; & en meme tems remercier le tout puissant de la Grace qu'il vous a fait de n'être point dans le triste Etat où il a reduit ces Infortunés. Vous donnerez en sortant chacun un Sou au Portier.

Tout au haut de ces Prez est la Pest-House, ou l'Hopital de François, c'est aussi leur Maison des Foux. Si vous voulez y aller vous le pourez, & en suite vous faire mener a l'Hopital d'Hoxton, qui en est tout proche, appellé Aske's Hopital, a fondé pour y loger & entretenir 20 pouvres Hommes ayant Maitrise dans la Compagnie des Chapeliers.

Magnifique Fondation pour un Particulier; mais qu'il n'a faite que par suppose Vanité, veu que dans

only out of Vanity, seeing that at the same time he provided against the Wants of those of the Company he was a Member of, he left his nearest Relations in Poverty and Misery. What a prodigious excess of Folly was this! The Square and Streets near this Hospital are very neat and pretty handsome, and the Country very agreeable.

From hence, if you think fit, you'll go to the Foundery which is at the upper-end of *Moorfields*, it is the place where all the Cannon and Mortars of *England* are Cast. When you come out you must give the Workmen something to drink. Afterwards returning towards the City you may go to the *Dutch* Church, which is as large as some Cathedrals. Near this is the *South-Sea-House*, which is now rebuilding and will be extraordinary fine. In the same Street, and nearer to *Moorfields* or *London-Wall*, is the Pay-Office for the Admiralty. And in the same Street Dra-

dans le tems qu'il pourvoyoit au besoins de ceux de la Compagnie dont il etoit Membre, il a laissé ses proches Parens dans la Pauvretté & dans la Misere. Quel excés de Folie! Le Quarré & les Ruës qui sont proche de cet Hopital sont très propres & assez Belles, & le Passage fort agreeable.

Dela, si vous le trouvez à propos, vous irez a la Fonderie qui est au haut de Moorfields, c'est le lieu ou l'on fabrique tous les Canons & Mortiers d'Angleterre. En sortant il faut donner quelque chose pour boire aux Ouvriers. Ensuite retournant vers la Ville vous pouvez aller à l'Eglise Hollandois, qui est aussi grande & aussi belle que quelque Cathedrales. Proche de la est la Maison de la Compagnie du Sud que l'on rebatit & qui sera extraordinairement belle. Dans la Même Ruë & plus proche des Moorfields où des murailles de Londres est le Bureau de la Paye pour l'Amirauté. Et dans

Drapers-Hall, which has a very fine Garden, where any one may take a Walk. Nearer the *Royal Exchange* in *Threadneedle-ftreet* is the old *French* Church which the *French* and *Walloons* call the *London* Church. The Service there is after the Way of the *Calvinifts*, as that of the *Dutch* is alfo: The *French* have the *Englifh* Service and Liturgy at St. *Martin Orgars* near *Cannon-ftreet*, and at feveral other Chapels; but the *Dutch* have the fame only in their own Language at the *French* and *Dutch* Chapel in St. *James's-Houfe*. In *Bifhopsgate-ftreet* is the Noble College founded by Sir *Thomas Grefham*, and which we have mention'd before. Here was formerly a very good Collection of Rarities; but they have been remov'd from thence to a Houfe in *Crane-Court* in *Fleet-ftreet*, where the Curious may fee them if they pleafe.

We might now fpeak of the feveral Churches, and alfo Halls of the 72 Com-

la même Rue la Halle des *Drapiers*, qui a un tres *Jardin*, ou l'on fe promêne. Plus près de la *Bourfe-Royal* & dans *Threadneedle-ftreet* eft la Vielle Eglife *Françoife*, que les *Françoife* & *Wallons*, appellent l'Eglife de *Londres*. Le Service s'y fait à la maniere des *Calviniftes*, auffi bien qu'a l' *Hollandoife*. Les *Françoife* ont le Service & la Liturgie à l' *Anglicane* a St. *Martin Orgars* & a plufieurs autres *Chapelles*, mais les *Hollandoife* ne l'ont en leur Langue qu'a la Chapelle *Hollandoife* au Palais de St. *James*. Dans la Rue de *Bifhops-gate* eft le Noble College fondé par le Chevalier *Thomas Grefham*, dont nous avons parlé cy devant. Il y avoit là autrefois un tres bon Recueil de Raretés, mais on les en a otées & difpofées dans une Maifon en *Crane-Court* dans *Fleet-ftreet*, où les Curieux les peuvent aller voir s'il leur plaît.

Nous pourions parler icy des differentes Eglifes, auffi bien que des Halles des

Companies of Trades and Merchants of this Great City, but the compass of this Volume cannot permit us to do it here: All we can say of them in general is, that the Churches are fine, convenient, and decently Magnificent; and that most of the Halls are large enough to be Palaces for Princes, and sumptuous and commodious enough to entertain Kings, leaving it to the Curiosity of Strangers to view them if they think fit.

From *Draper's-Hall* you may go to view *Blackwel-Hall*, where you will be surprised to see the vast quantity of Woollen-Cloth, Drugget, and Stuffs that are deposited and sold there.

Thence you may go through *Aldermanbury* to *Sion-College*, where you will see a fine Publick Library: Those who will have the use of it must give three or four Shillings for their Inscription. After this you may go to the

72 *Compagnies de Metiers & de Negoce de cette Grande Ville, mais le peu d'etenduë de ce Volume ne nous permet pas: Tout ce que nous en pouvons dire en General c'est que les Eglises sont belles Commodes & Magnifiques avec Decence: Et que la plus part des Halles sont Grandes assez pour servir de Palais a un Prince, & assez somptueuses & commodes pour y regaler des Rois, nous laissons a la Curiosité des Etrangers de les voir s'ils le trouvent a propos.*

De Draper's-Hall, vous pouvez aller voir Blackwel-Hall, ou vous serez surpris de voir la quantité de Laines de Draps, de Droggets, & d'Etoffes qui s'y deposent & s'y vendent.

De là vous irez par Aldermanbury au Collège de Sion, vous y verrez une tres belle Bibliotheque Publique, ceux qui voudront en avoir l'usage ou le privilege donneront trois ou quatres Chellins au Bibliothequaire pour leur Inscription. Apres cela vous ferez conduire à la

F 3   *Charter-*

Charter-House.

IT is a great and spacious Hospital founded by *Robert Sutton*, Esq; Partner and intimate Friend of Sir *Thomas Gresham*; there are here 40 Scholars who are maintain'd and instructed *gratis*; beside 80 old Gentlemen, who are maintain'd there also, that is, cloathed, lodged and fed, and to whom the Founder has also provided a handsom weekly Pocket-Allowance for their odd Expences. There are fine Walks and Allies in this Place, very neat Lodgings; and, in short, the Grandeur and Magnificence of this Hospital, and of this Foundation, are so considerable, that the Kings and greatest Lords of this Kingdom are commonly Governors thereof. He who is the Master or Director of it (and who, by order of the Founder, must be a Clergyman) has 500 *l.* per

Charter-House.

C'Est un vaste & grand Hôpital fondé par Monsieur Robert Sutton, Associé & Ami intime du Chevalier Thomas Gresham; il y a icy 40 Echoliers qui sont entretenus & instruits gratis, outre 80 vieux Gentilshommes, que l'on y habille, loge, & nourit; & auxquels le Fondateur a aussi pourvu une bonnete Allouance, par semaines pour leurs menu Plaisirs, ou leurs autres Necessitez. Il y a de belles Promenades, des Allées d'Arbres, des Logemens très propres, enfin la Grandeur & la Magnificence de cet Hôpital & de cette Fondation, sont si considérables que les Rois & les plus Grands Seigneurs du Royaume en sont ordinairement Gouverneurs. Celui qui en est le Directeur & qui par Ordre du Fondateur est toujours un Ecclesiastique, a 500 Livres Sterlin de Rente. Cet Hôpi-

per *An.* This Hospital is situated in a good Air, and has every thing that is agreeable and convenient for Life within itself, or belonging to it. Its yearly Income amounts to about 10000 *l.*

From hence you may go to *Smithfield,* it is the greatest Market in *England* for Horses and Cattle: You'll find at all times Horses to be bought there, but you must take care to examine them well, for the Jockies are errant Cheats. In the middle of this Market there is a Ring of large Stones; it was in the middle of this Ring that the Martyrs of the Protestant Religion were burnt, in the Reign of cruel Queen *Mary.* Near this Place you see a fine Frontispiece, which is that of St. *Bartholomew's* Hospital; above the Gate you see the Statue of King *Henry* VIII who repair'd, or rebuilt it, as the Inscription below the Statue tells you: On the Left-hand and in the Entry is the Church: The

Hopital est scitué dans un bon Air, & a en soi & a soi tout ce qui est agreable & commode à la Vie. Son Revenu se monte à près de dix Mille Livres Sterlin.

De là faites vous conduire a Smithfield, c'est le plus grand Marché de l'Angleterre pour les Chevaux & le Betail. Vous y trouverés en tout tems des Chevaux a acheter mais il faut se donner grand Soin de les bien examiner, car les Matignons sont de maitres Trompeurs. Dans le milieu de ce Marché on void un Rond de Pierres; c'est au milieu de ce rond que l'on bruloit les Martyrs de la Religion Protestante du tems de la cruelle Reine Marie. Près de là on void un beau Frontispice qui est celui de l'Hopital de St. Bartholomée au dessus de la Porte se voit la Statue du Roj Henry *VIII, qui la refondé, comme le dit l'Inscription qui est dessous la Statue. A Coté & dans l'entrée est l'Eglise. La grand*

Salle

The Great Hall is on both sides fill'd with fine Shops. Go through this Hall and follow the Passage at the end of it and it will bring you to

Christ - Church Hospital,

COmmonly called *The Blew-Coat-Boys Hospital*, because they are dress'd in that Colour. This Hospital was founded by King *Edward* VI. for decay'd Freemens Sons and Daughters; there are about a Thousand Boys and Girls who are very well Cloathed and Maintained here, and who, as soon as they are thirteen or fourteen Years old, are put out Apprentices for Seven Years, and when they are out of their Times they have a certain Sum of Money to help them to setup. As there have been some Lord Mayors, Aldermen, &c. who had been brought up in this Hospital, so they have left considerable Legacies to it

Salle est remplie de belles Boutiques. Passez a travers de cette Salle, & suivez le Passage qui est au bout, & il vous menera à

L' Hopital de l' Eglise de Christ,

COmmunement appellé L'Hopital des Enfans Blew, parce qu'ils sont Habillé de cette Couleur là. Cet Hopital a eté fondé par le Roy Edouard VI. pour les Orphelins dont les Peres avoient Droit de Maitrise dans la Cité de Londres, il y en a près de Mille Garçons & Filles, qui sont tres bien nouris & entretenus & qui dès qu'ils ont treize a quatorze Ans, sont mis en Apprentissage pour les Sept Ans, apres quoi on leur donne une certaine Somme pour les aider à s'etablir. Comme il y a souvent eu des Lords Maires, des Aldermen, &c. qui avoient eté elevé dans cet Hopital, il lui ont fait des Legs & Donations tres Considerables à leur Mort.

Il

it at their Deaths. Here is also a School for Mathematicks and Navigation, founded by King *Charles* II. One may go of a *Sunday* to see these Children eat, and you'll be surprised at the fine Order and Neatness that is observed at their Meals. Going from this Place through the Gate that brings you to *Newgate-street*, you'll see in a Nich the Statue of the Founder King *Edward* VI. But in case you go out of the other Gate that goes into the same Street you'll see the Statue of K. *Charles* II.

Cross *Newgate-street* and enter into *Warwick-lane* and you'll see the *College of Physicians*; it is a fine Building with a stately Cupola. It is in this College that the Anatomical Dissections are made: There is this Inscription:

Omnis Cutleri cedat Labor Amphitheatro.

Here is a large and magnificent Hall, where the Physicians meet; and as *Charles*

Il y a aussi une Echole de Mathematiques & de Navigation fondée par Charles II. On peut aller voir Manger ces Enfans, & on sera charmé du bel Ordre & de la propreté qui s'observe a leurs Repas. En sortant delà par la Porte qui mene a Newgate-street vous voyez dans une Niche la Statuë du Fondateur le jeune Roy Edouard VI. Mais si vous sortez par l'autre Porte qui conduit a la Meme Ruë vous y verrez celle de Charles II.

Traversez la Ruë de Newgate & entrez dans Warwick-lane & vous y verrez le College de Medicins; c'est un trés bel Ediffice avec un beau Dome. C'est dans ce College que l'on fait les Dissections Anatomiques: On y voit cette Inscription:

Omnis Cutleri cedat Labor Amphitheatro.

Il y icy une grand & magnifique Sale ou les Medicins s'assemblent, & comme Charles

Charles II. was a Benefactor to this College, they have placed his Statue in it with an Inscription. You must give something to the Warder, who will also give you a List or Catalogue of the Incorporate and Honorary Physicians.

Thence you go to *Newgate*, which is the Prison of Criminals, tho' there are also Prisoners for Debt. You see on the Inside *Justice* holding a Sword in her Hand, and *Strength* and *Prudence* on each side of her. On the Outside there are four Figures imboss'd, the first is *Liberty* holding a Hat in her Hand with this Motto, *Libertas*. The second is *Peace* holding a Dove in her Hand and a Helmet under her Feet. The third is *Severity*, holding a bundle of Rods in her Hand. And the fourth is *Plenty*, holding a Horn of Plenty in her Hand. Near the top of the Gate on that side there is a Sun-Dial with this Motto, *Venio ut fur*, alluding to the Thieves who

Charles II. a été Bienfaiteur a ce College, on y a placé sa Statue, avec une Inscription. Il faut donner quelque chose au Gardien qui vous donnera aussi le Catalogue des Medicins Aggregé & Honoraires.

De la vous irez a la Porte de *Newgate*, qui est la Prison des Criminels, quoi qu'il y ait aussi des Prisoniers pour Debtes. On voit au dedans la *Justice* tient l'Epée a la Main, & la Prudence & la Force a coté d'elle. Au dehors il y a quatres Figures en Bosse; la première tient un Chapeau a la Main avec cette Devise *Libertas*. La seconde est la Paix, elle tient une Colombe a la Main & a un Casque sous ses Pieds. La troisieme est la Sévérité, elle tient un faisceau de Verges. La quatrieme est la Abondance tient une Corne d'Abondance. Au haut de cette Porte il y a un Quadran au Soleil avec cette Devise, *Venio ut fur*, faisant allusion au Voleurs qui y viennent inopi-

who come there unexpected, as the Sun, and disappear as its Shadow. If you come near the Thieves, either Men or Women, you must be very cautious, for they are very dextrous in picking of Pockets. When there are any who have receiv'd Sentence of Death, you may go to *Newgate* of a *Sunday* Morning when they come to hear Sermon in the Chapel, you must give the Goalers something to Drink before they let you in. View the several Places within this Prison.

When you are come out of this frightful Purgatory, you may go view the Sessions-House in the *Old-Baily*, where they try the Malefactors.

You may go afterwards to *Holbourn*, where on your Left-hand you see St. *Andrew*'s Church, which is very fine. On the Right-hand you come to *Ely-House*, where the Bishops of *Ely* reside, and which belongs to that Diocese, tho' in the City of

inopinément comme le Soleil & passent comme son Ombre. Si vous approchez des voleurs, soit Homme soit Femme, il faut bien prendre garde à vous, car ils sont extremement subtils à vuider les Poches. Lors qu'il y en a qui ont reçu Sentence de Mort, on y peut aller le Dimanche Matin qu'ils viennent entendre le Sermon dans la Chapelle, & on donne quelque Chose au Geolier pour y entrer. Visité tous les Endroits de cette Prison.

Quand vous serez sorti de cet affreux Purgatoire vous pourrez aller voir la Maison de la Session, où l'on juge les Malfaiteures.

Ensuite vous vous ferez conduire en Holbourn où vous trouverez a Gauche l'Eglise de St. André, qui est très belle. A Droite vous trouvé la Maison d'Ely, Residence des Eveques d'Ely, & qui est de ce Diocese quoique dans Londres:

C'est

of *London* : It is an ancient Palace, very spacious, and there is a pretty good Chapel.

Then going on to the West, you find on your Right-hand *Furnival's-Inn*; (the Lawyers call Inns the Places where they have Chambers, where they keep their Offices.) The most considerable you come next to is

Gray's-Inn.

THere are fine Courts, a Chapel, a Library, and an extraordinary fine and spacious Garden, where People walk under fine Trees and in very agreeable Walks. It is behind this Garden that one of the new additional Buildings made to this large Metropolis begins, and which consists of several Streets, and 2 Churches; the Streets are neat, strait and magnificent. If you return from *Gray's-Inn* into *Holbourn* you come a little higher into *Chancery-*

C'est un ancienne Palais, tres spacieux, où il y a une assez belle Chapelle.

De la en montant toujours vers l'Occident vous trouvez a Droite Furnival's-Inn (les *Jurisconsultes* appellent Inn les endroits où ils ont des Chambres où ils tiennent leurs Bureaux). Delà vous viendrez a

Gray's-Inn.

OU il y a une Chapelle, une Bibliotheque, de belles Cours & un tres beau & spacieux Jardin, où l'on se promene sous de belles Allées d'Arbres & dont les Promenades sont tres belles. C'est derriere ce Jardin que commence l'un des Quartiers qu'on nouvellement batis; & qui consiste en plusieurs nouvelles Ruës, & 2 nouvelle Eglises; les Ruës y sont tres propres droites & magnifiques. Si vous ventrez dans la grande Ruë de Holbourn en sortant de Gray's-Inn vous entrerez

un

cery-lane, and at the end of a long Wall on the West of the said Street is

Lincoln's-Inn,

WHich has a very fine Chapel, and the Windows of it are very finely painted. The Court of this Inn, which is called *Lincoln's-Inn New-Square*, is very fine, in the middle of this Court is a Fountain, in which there is a Pillar with a Clock and Dial on the top of it. The Stamp-Office is in this Square, the King's-Arms are above the Door of this Office. On the North of this Square there is a magnificent Garden free to all Persons above the inferior Rank to walk in. It has fine Walks, Statues, &c. Coming out of this Garden towards the West you come to the fine Square of *Lincoln's-Inn-Fields*, which, next to the Place of St. *Mark* at *Venice,*

un peu plus haut dans Chancery-lane, *& vous trouverez au bout d'une grande Muraille, qui est a l'Occident de la dite Rüe,*

Lincoln's-Inn,

DOnt la Chapelle est tres Belles, les fenetres en sont tres bien Peintés. Le Cour de cet Inn qu'on appelle Lincoln's-Inn New-Square, est tres belle, il y a une Fontaine au milieu dans laquelle, il y a une Colomne où il y a une Horologe. Le Bureau du Papier Timbré est dans cette cour & les Armes d'Angleterre sont au dessus de la Porte de ce Bureau. Au Nord de cette Cour il y a un magnifique Jardin Public où les Personnes au dessus du Commun ont la Liberté de se promener. Il y a de belles Promenades, des Statues, &c. En sortant de ce Jardin vous allez toujours vers l'Occident & vous entré dans le beau Quarré de le Lincoln's-Inn-Fields, qui est une des plus grandes Places *de*

Venice, is the largest in *Europe*. On the South of it there is an Entry to the Playhouse: And on the West-end is *Lindsey-House*, belonging to the Duke of *Ancaster* and *Kestevan*. On the Corner to the South of the said West-end is the Lord Chancellor's; and within three Doors of that is the House of the *Sardinian* Embassador, where the *Roman* Catholicks have the finest Chapel for their Worship in *England*. And on the Corner to the North is the House of the Duke of *Newcastle*, His Majesty's Principal Secretary of State. Coming out of this Square to the North you cross *Holbourn* again, and go to view *Red-Lion-Square*, which is very pretty and surrounded with fine Buildings, as well as *Lincoln's-Inn* and *Lincoln's-Inn-Fields*. From hence you go behind *Gray's-Inn* and see the fine Cock-Pit there. And following the New Buildings you'll go directly to *Queen* Anne's Square; on the West of which

de l'Europe après la Place de St. Marc à Venice. Au Midy il y a une Entrée a la Comedie; & a l'Occident de cette place est l'Hotel de Lindsey, appartenant au Duc de Ancaster & de Kestevan. Au Coin au Midy est celui du Lord Chancelier; & a trois Portes de la est l'Hotel de l'Ambassadeur de Sardaigne, où est a present la plus belle Chapelle pour les Catholique Romaine qu'il y ait en Angleterre. Et au Coin au Nord est celui du Duc de Newcastle, Secretaire d'Etat. En sortant de ce Quarré vers le Nord vous retournés traverser Holbourn, & passerez au Red-Lion-Square, qui est fort beau & environné de belles Maisons aussi bien que Lincoln's-Inn & Lincolns's-Inn Fields. De la vous allez derrière Gray's-Inn, où vous verrez un beau Cock-Pit. De la vous allez tout droit vers ce qu'on appelle le Quarré de la Reine Anne; à l'Occident du quel est l'Eglise de

which is St. *George's* Church, the Inside of which is very fine. And on the East is *Ormond-street*, where you ought not to omit to see the fine House of the Lord *Powis*, the Front of it is all of Free-stone, and the Architecture of an admirable Beauty; the Apartments are Magnificent, Beautiful, Commodious and well Lighted: Its Prospect from the Front is confin'd, but it has one of the finest Prospects in *London* from its Back-Windows. There is a Phœnix reviving from its Ashes above the Door on the Front, in allusion that this House which was reduced to Ashes when the Duke *d'Aumont* dwelt in it, has been rebuilt with more Magnificence than it had before. Thence go to the West and you will come to *Southampton-Row* which is a Row of Houses newly built, and which is very regular.

Thence you go towards *Bloomsbury-Square*; which is a pretty handsome one, on the North of which

de St. George, dont l'Interieur est tres beau. Et à l'Orient Ormond-street, où vous irez voir la Maison du Lord **Powis**, dont le Frontispice est tout de Pierre de Taille, & l'Architecture d'un Gout admirable; les Appartemens en sont Magnifiques, Beaux, Commodes, & bien Eclairés, sa Vuë est bornée sur le Devant, mais sur le derriere, elle a une des plus belles Vuës de Londres. Au haut de la Porte il y a un Phænix qui renait de ses Cendres: Faisant allusion à ce que cet Hotel qui fut reduit en Cendres lors que le Feu Duc d'Aumont y Logeoit a été Reedifié avec plus de Magnificence qu'il n'en avoit auparavant. De la Montez vers l'Occident & vous viendrez en Southampton-Row, qui est une Rangée de Maisons Nouvellement batie & qui est tres Reguliere.

De la vous monterez vers Bloomsbury-Square, qui est un quarrez assez Joli, dans lequel est l'Hotel

which is *Southampton-House*, belonging to the Duke of *Bedford*. You see the Gardens of it from *Southampton-Row*.

Going on to the West you will come to the magnificent *Montague-House*, the late Lord of that Name built it, and spared no Cost to render it the most Beautiful in *London* : It is a very regular Building, and of a most excellent Architecture. In short, to give you a just Idea of it, it is sufficient to tell you, that the Families of the present Duke, and my Lord his late Father's were lodged in the Wings of this House at the same time, tho' they were the largest Families in *England*; and that the Body of this House is the finest and most spacious in *London*. Behind this House is a very fine Garden adorn'd with Statues.

From this you may go to see the new Church which is in *Bloomsbury-Market*; the Frontispiece of it is very fine, as well

as

Hotel de Southampton, appartenant au Duc de Bedford. Et dont vous voyez les Jardins de Southamton-Row.

En montant vers l'Occident vous viendrez au magnifique Hotel de Montague, le feu Lord de ce Nom la fait batir & n'a rien Epargné pour le rendre un des plus magnifiques de Londres : C'est un Batiment fort regulier & d'une tres excellente Architecture. Enfin pour vous en donner une juste Idée, il suffit de dire, que les Ailes de la Maison ont contenu la Familles du present Duc & celle de mi Lord son Pere quoy qu'elles etoient des plus grandes d'Angleterre, & que le Corps du Logis est un des plus Beaux & des plus spacieux de Londres. Il y a derriere cet Hotel un beau Jardin orné de Statues.

De la vous pourrez aller voir la nouvelle Eglise qui est dans le Marché de Bloomsbury ; le Frontispice en est tres beau

as its Steeple, on the top of which they have whimsically put King *George*'s Statue, which is tollerably well done, and is 17 Foot high.

Thence you may go by broad St. *Giles*'s to *Monmouth-street*, and so to the Seven-Dials, which is a Pillar to which seven Streets terminate. And from thence you'll go to *Soho*-Square, this Square as well as those of *Leicester*-Fields, *Red-Lion*-Square, *Hanover*-Square, and *Cavendish*-Square is paled about. In the middle of this Square is the Statue of King *Charles* II. on the East there is a very fine House, which formerly belong'd to the D. of *Monmouth*, and now belongs to the Lord Viscount *Bateman*. It is on the Corner to the West of this House that Count *Broglio*, Ambassador of *France*, now lodges : This Square is very fine.

From hence you'll go to *Poland* and *Marlborough*-Streets, which are very

beau aussi bien que sa Tour, sur le haut de la quelle on s'est avisé de placer la Statuë du Roy George, qui est assez bien faite & a dix sept Pieds de haut.

De la vous pourez vous faire mener par Monmouth-street, *aux* Seven-Dials, *que l'on appelle en Françoise la Pyramide a la quelle sept Ruës viennent aboutir. Et ensuite vous vous ferez mener au Quarré de* Monmouth, *qu'on appelle aussi le Quarré de* Soho, *ce Quarré icy, aussi bien que ceux de* Leicester-Fields, Red-Lion-Square, Hanover-Square, *&* Cavendish Square, *est entourré de Pallisades, au milieu de ce Quarré est la Statuë Pedestre de* Charles II. *a l'Orient est un tres bel Hotel qui appartenoit autrefois au Duc de* Monmouth *& qui appartient a present a* Mr. le Vicomt Bateman. *C'est sur le Coin a l'Occident de cet Hotel où loge a present* Mr. le Comte de Broglio *Ambassadeur de* France : *Ce Quarré est tres beau.*

De la vous vous ferez conduire a Poland *&* Marlborough-Streets, *qui sont*

G   *de*

very fine Streets. Then turning a little to the South you may go to *Golden*-Square, but it is not so fine as the two former. Then you may go by *King-street* to *Cavendish-Square*, where you will see very fine Buildings, but which are not yet finish'd. Here begins what they call the *New-Buildings*, and here you shall see enough to satisfy your Curiosity, both with respect to the Largeness, Beauty, Magnificence, and Regularity of the Houses, even the smallest of them. Every Street deserves to be seen, especially those near *Hanover*-Square and *Burlington*-Garden, where they have lately built Houses as large and as sumptuous as Palaces. Go also to see *Burlington*-House, which is very magnificent: My Lord *Burlington* who is very well skill'd in Pictures, *&c.* is making a Collection of them, which is already a good one. Then you may go see *Devonshire*-House, which is also a very fine House;

de tres belles Ruës. Vous pourrez en vous detournant un peu voir le *Quarré de Or*, mais il n'est pas si beau que les deux premiers. Puis vous irez par King-street voir le *Quarré de Cavendish*, ou vous verrez de magnifiques Hotels, mais qui ne sont pas encore finis. C'est icy où commence ce qu'on appelle les Nouveaux Batimens, & où vous trouverez dequoi vous satisfaire, soit pour la Grandeur, la Beauté, la Magnificence, & la Regularité des Hotels, & même des moindres Maisons. Chaque Ruë merite d'être vuë, sur tout celles qui sont près d' Hanover-Square & de Burlington-Garden, c'est a dire Jardins de Burlington, où l'on a depuis peu fait plusieurs Ruës & Batis des Hotels aussi grands & aussi superbe que des Palais : quand vous les aurez vu, allez aussi voir l'Hotel de Burlington, qui est tres magnifique. My Lord Burlington qui se connoit tres bien en Tableaux, en fait une Collection qui est deja assez bonné. De la voir pourrez aller voir celui du

Duc

House; and do not omit to see His Grace the Duke of *Devonshire's* fine Collection of Paintings, which is the best in *England.* If you please you may go see a great many Statues at the Statuaries at *Hide-Park* Corner. And from thence return by *Arlington*-Street to St. *James's*-Street, view St. *James's*-Square, and reserve your Walks to the Places without the City to another Time.

We omitted (because we would not carry you too much out of the way of the most remarkable Places) to mention *Wapping, Southwark,* the fine Street and Parts of *Goodman's-Fields, White-Chapel, Spittle-Fields,* which is the Hamlet where the most part of the Weavers live, and where they have lately built whole Streets that are very fine ; also *Clerkenwel,* St. *John's,* which formerly was the Place of Residence and House of the Knighs of St. *John* of *Jerusalem,* and of which some Ruins are yet

Duc de Devonshire, *qui est tres beau ; n'oubliez pas de voir la belle Collection de Peintures de Monseigneur le Duc de* Devonshire, *qui est la meilleure de l'*Angleterre. *Si vous le souhaité vous pourrez aller voir plusieurs Statuës qui sont chez les Statuaires a* Hide-Park Corner. *Et de la revenir par* Arlington-Street *dans* St. James's-Street, *voir le Quarré de St.* James, *& vous reserver avoir les Lieux hors de la Ville une autrefois.*

Pour ne vous point trop detourner nous avons omis de vous parler de Wapping, *de* Southwark, *des belles Ruës & du beau Quartier de* Goodmans-Fields, *de* White-Chapel, *du* Spittle-Fields, *qui est le Quartier des Ouvriers en soye & des Tisserans, & ou on a depuis peu bati des Ruës entieres qui sont tres belles ; de* Clerkenwel, *de* St. John's, *qui etoit autrefois le Lieu de Residence & Hotel des Chevaliers de St.* Jean *de* Jerusalem, *& dont on voit encore les Ruïnes. Mais*

yet to be feen; we fhall speak of them when we direct you to the pleafant Villages and Places about *London*; and it is almoft impoffible to defcribe all the Particulars and Beauties of this Great City, fince it is computed it has above 5000 Streets, 12 great Squares, and feveral leffer ones, and near 130000 Inhabitants; that there are 96 Parifhes within the Bounds of the City only, and that there are in all above 130 Parifhes in the City and Suburbs, befides above 200 Chapels and Conventicles, without including thofe of the *Roman Catholicks*, the Grecians, Armenians, Jews, &c. We fhall here give you a fhort defcription of the Places abovenamed, beginning by

mais nous en parlerons en vous conduifant aux Villages & Endroits agreables qui font aux environs de Londres; *& il eft impoffible de marquer toutes les Particularités & les Beautés de cette Grand Ville, puis qu'on y comte plus de 5000 Rües, 12 grand Quarrez, & plufieurs moindres, & pres de 130000 Habitants, qu'il y a 96 Eglifes Paroiffiales dans la feule Enceinte de la Cité, & qu'il y en a en tout plus de 130 dans la Ville & les Fauxbourgs outre plus de 200 Chapelles ou Conventicules, fans compter celles des* Catholiques Romains, *des* Grecs, Armeniens, Juifs, *&c. Nous donnerons icy une Relation en abregé des Endroits fufdits commençant par*

Wapping.

Wapping.

AS foon as you are beyond the *Tower* going down the River, you come to St. *Catherines*, and when you have paffed

DEs que l'on a paffé la Tour de Londres en defcendant la Riviere vous venez a Ste. Catherine & apres que vous avez

passed a Bridge called *Hermitage-Bridge*, you come into *Wapping*. It is a very large, rich and populous Suburb ; here the moft part of the Captains, or Mafters of Trading Ships and Veffels, and their Sailors dwell : It is near two Miles long. Then you come to *Shadwel*, which is along the River. Then you come to *Ratcliffe*, and then to *Limehoufe*, which is reckon'd about four Miles from *London - Bridge*. Thefe four Places are contiguous, and they contain fo many little Lanes, Allies, and Courts, that they fwarm with People, and are fo confiderable that they contain as many Houfes as feveral Capital Cities do, tho' there is no very remarkable Buildings there.

avez paſſez un Pont qu'on appelle le Pont de l' Hermitage vous entrez Wapping. *C'eſt un Fauxbourg tres grand, tres rich, & tres Peuplé ; c'eſt là que la pluspart des Capitaines & Matelots des vaiſſeaux Marchands demeurent. Il a pres d'une Lieuë d'etenduë. Apres cela on trouve* Shadwel, *qui eſt auſſi au bord de la Riviere. Enſuite on vient a* Ratcliffe, *& puis a* Limehoufe, *qu'on eſtime etre a plus de quatre Milles du Pont de* Londres. *Ces quartiers ont un nombre infini de petites Ruës & petites Cours, qui fourmillent de Monde, & ſont ſi Conſiderables qu'ils contiennent autant de Maiſons que pluſieurs Villes Capitales, quos quil n'y a pas d'édifice fert conſiderable.*

The Borough of Southwark.

Le Bourg de Southwark.

THe Bridge of *London* makes it contiguous to this City, which, with the great Trade

LE Pont de Londres *le rend contigu a la Ville, ce qui joint au grand Negoce que ſa Scituation*

Trade it has by its being situated near the River, and the great number of Coaches, Carriages, and Cattle that pass through it, have so far enlarg'd it, that altho' it is not the County Town of the Shire, yet it is much larger than *Kingston*, which is the Capital of that County. In this Borough is St. *Thomas*'s Hospital, wherein they admit the Sick from all Parts of the Town, when they are recommended by one of the Governors of the said Hospital. But this, as large and well endowed as it is, will be nothing in comparison to that which is now building there, and which will cost 50000 *l.* building, and will have above 10000 *l. per Ann.* and where all Incurables will be admitted, taken care of, and maintain'd on the Income of the Hospital. The most surprising thing of it is, that a private Person, who was sometime ago a Bookseller, named Mr. *Guy*, was the Founder, who

tuation sur le Bord de la Riviere lui attire & au grand nombre de Carosses, Voitures & Bestiaux qui y passent l'ont si fort augmenté que quoi qu'il ne soit pas la Capitale de la Province de Surrey, *il est beaucoup plus grand que* Kingston, *Capitale de la dite Province. C'est dans ce Bourg qu'est l'Hopital de St.* Thomas, *où l'on reçoit les Malades qui viennent de tous les Endroits de la Ville. Mais qui tout grand & bien doüé qu'il est ne sera pas grand chose en Comparaison de celui que l'on y batit a present & que coutera* 50000 *Livres Sterlin a batir & aura* 10000 *Livres Sterlin de Rente, & où tous les Malades Incurables seront receus, nouris, traité, & entretenus sur le fond de l'Hopital. Ce qu'il y a de plus surprenant c'est, que c'est un simple particulier cy devant Marchand Libraire nommé* Mr. Guy, *qui en est le fondateur & qui a donné* 250000 *Livres Sterlin,*

who has given 25000 *l.* to build it and settle this Revenue on it; which is a Foundation great enough for a Sovereign Prince. You have also in this Borough the Court of the

Sterlin, pour le batir & pour lui etablir le dit Revenu; C'est dans ce Bourg qu'est aussi la Prison du

King's-Bench,

WHere Prisoners are put for great Debts, and where some buy the Liberty of the Rules of that Prison, whereby they may walk over all St. George's-Fields. And there are some who being unable to pay all their Debts keep in their hands what small Stock they have saved from the merciless Greediness of their Creditors, and spend here the remainder of their Days. Next to it you come to the Prison of the

Banc du Roy,

OU l'on mett les Prisoniers pour de Grosses, & où il y en a qui achettent la Liberté du Domaine de la Prison, par où ils peuvent aller par tous les Prez de St. George; & il y en a qui ne pouvant payer toutes leur Dettes, retiennent le peu de Fond qu'ils ont sauvé de l'Avidité cruelle de leurs Creanciers, & passent icy le reste de leurs Jours. Tout à tenant est la Prison de la

Marshalsea,

WHere (by the inhumane Law that allows that a Person be detain'd even before the Debt

Marechaussée,

OU (par la detestable Loy qui donne Prise de Corps avant même que la Dette soit prouvée)

G 4

il

Debt is prov'd) a number of miserable Insolvents are detain'd for trifling Debts, or at least of very small Consequence; so that many a poor Man or Woman who is put in here for Half a Crown, or Five Shillings, has been forced to perish therein, or to stay there till charitable Persons pay their Fees, which amount to 15 s. besides what Debts they are obliged to contract with the Goaler to hinder themselves from starving: and which sometimes amount to three times as much, and must absolutely be paid before they can be enlarged.

There is a very considerable Market, and a very good Trade in this Borough, as also several Wharfs, and Docks to build Ships and Barks, and two fine Glass-houses that are worthy of your sight, and four or five Churches; near that of St. *George* are the fine Meadows call'd S.*George's Fields*, and which reach to *Lambeth-House*, which we

il y a une infinité de Miserables detenus pour des Dettes de Rien ou de tres petites Consequences de sorte que tel pauvre Homme ou Femme qui y a eté mis pour 30 Sols ou un Ecu, ou même pour de simples Paroles, a eté contraint d'y perir, ou d'y rester jusqu'a ce que des Personnes Charitables en ayent payé les fraix qui se montent à trois Ecus outre les Dettes qu'ils sont obligés de contracter au Geolier pour s'empecher de mourir de faim; & qui se montent quelques fois a deux ou trois fois autant; & qu'il leur faut payer absolument avant de pouvoir etre Liberés.

Il y a dans ce Bourg un Marché considerable, & un tres bon Negoce plusieurs Quais & Chantiers a batir des Vaisseaux & des Barques, deux belles Verreries qui meritent d'etre Vuë; & quatre ou cinq grandes & belles Eglises; tout proche de celle de St. George font les Belles Prairies qu'on appelle St. George's-Fields, & qui vous mement au Palais Ar-

we shall speak of by and by. There is also *Cupids Garden* in the same Fields, which you must not omit to see. Near the *Tower* of *London* are the handsome Parts called

Archiepiscopal de **Lambeth** *(dont nous parlerons cy apres) aussi bien qu'a* Cupid's-Garden, *c'est une tres agreable Promenade dont il ne faut pas manquer de se donner le plaisir de les voir. Vous pourrez au sortir de la* Tour *de Londres, aller par les Minories au Quartier de*

Goodman's-Fields,

Goodmans-Fields,

WHere are very fine Streets, fine Buildings and very regular, but otherwise nothing remarkable. From hence you may go to *White-Chapel,* and see the Church, the Altar and Pulpit of which are very fine. Thence you may go to *Mile-end,* where on the Road you see an Hospital for Sea-Captains Widows, where they have each an Apartment, and are very well maintain'd. Near this Place is *Bednal-Green,* famous for the Story of the Blind - Beggar thereof. And going on to the East you come to *Stepney,* which, as we said before,

is

OU il y a de tres belles Ruës de beaux Ediffices & tres reguliers, mais il n'y a outre cela rien de remarquable. De là on peut aller à White-Chapel, *& voir l' Eglise dont l' Autel, & la Chaire sont tres beaux. De la si vous le voulez vous pourrez aller à* Mile-end, *où sur le grand Chemin, vous voyez un Hôpital pour les Veuves des Capitaines de Vaisseaux, où elles ont chacune un Appartement, & sont tres bien entretenuës. Proche d'icy est* Bednal-Green, *fameux pour l' Histoire de son Mendicant-Aveugle. Et allant vers l'est vous venez à* Stepney, *qui comme nous l'avons dit*

est

is the Parish that the Hamlet of *Spittle-Fields* belongs to; there are good Buildings, pleasant Walks, here. And not far from hence is *Black-wall*, where they build Men of War. And as you return from hence, turning on your Right-hand at *Mile-end*, you come to

est la Paroisse dont le Spittle - Fields *depend ; il y a de beaux Batimens & de belles Promenades. Près de la est* Blackwal, *où l'on batit des Vaisseaux de Guerre. En Revenant De là & tournant à Droite a* Mile-end *vous entréz dans les*

Spittle-Fields,

Spittle-Fields,

IT is a vast and large Place, where they reckon there are above 100000 Silk, Plush, and Woolsted Weavers; it is the largest and most populous Parish in *Europe*, besides, as we formerly mention'd, the Church and Island of *St. Helens* near the Cape of *Good Hope* belongs to it. They have lately built a new Church there, which will be erected into a Parish and be dismember'd from the ancient Parish of *Stepney.*

C'*Est un vaste & grand Quartier où l'on compte qu'il y a plus de* 100000 *Ouvriers en Soye, en Peluche, en Cotton & en Laines ; & c'est la plus grand Paroisse & la plus Peuplée, qu'il y ait en Univers, outre que le E-glise l' Isle & de St.* He-lene *près du Cap de* Bon-ne *Esperance en depend. On y a bati depuis peu une nouvelle Eglise qui fera Paroisse & que l'on demembrera de l'ancienne Paroisse de* Stepney.

Hackney.

Hackney

IS within two Miles of *Spittle-Fields.* Many of the wealthy Citizens of *London* have built Houses here that look like Palaces, especially the Quakers, who have some here that are magnificent. You may another Day go to

Islington,

NEar this Village is a Place where People go to drink Mineral Waters, the Beer brewed there with this Water is very wholsome and purgative. Next to this Place is *Sadler's-Wells,* here you have, all the Summer, Rope-dancing, Vaulting on the Slack-Rope, Singing, *&c.* every Evening there is a Farce acted, which every Body may see paying only for the Wine you drink there. Not far from this Place is St. *John's,* and the Ruins of the Place of the

Hackney

ESt a deux Milles de Spittle-Fields. Beaucoup de riches Bourgeois de Londres y ont fait batir des Maisons qui ressemblent a des Palais, sur tout les Trembleurs, qui y en ont de magnifiques. Vous pourrez un autre jour vous faire mener a

Islington,

TOut près de ce Village il y a un endroit où l'on va boire des eaux Minerales, la Biere qu'on y boit & que l'on brasse de cette Eau, est tres saine & un peu purgative. Tout a coté de cet endroit est Sadler's-Wells, il y a des Danceurs de Corde, Voltigeurs, &c. & tous les Soirs dans la belle Saison, on y represente des Farces Divertissantes, que l'on void en payant seulement pour le Vin qu'on y boit. A peu de distance d'icy est St. John's, & les Ruines du Palais des Chevaliers de

the Knights of *Jerusalem*. And hard by this is the ancient Church of St. *James Clerkenwel*: there is nothing very particular to be seen at these two Places, except a fine new Street called *Red-Lion-street*, which is a very regular and beautiful Building.

Hamstead and *Highgate*

ARe two pretty Villages and very agreeably situated on two Hills within a Mile from each other, and each within four Miles of *London*; a great many Persons of Fashion go there to take the Air. Here are very fine Houses, and particularly *Bellsize*, where are fine Gardens, Horse-Races, &c. for the Diversion of those that go there to drink, &c. You may afterwards go to see the Hospital for Invalids called

de Jerusalem. *Et tout proche est l'ancienne Eglise de St. James Clerkenwel, il n'y a rien de fort particulier a voir en ces deux endroits, sice n'est la nouvelle Ruë appellée Red-Lion-street, qui est d'un Ouvrage fort regulier & fort beau.*

Hamstead and Highgate

SOnt *deux Villages tres agreables scitués sur deux Collines proche l'une de l'autre & Eloignées de quatre Milles de Londres, on y rencontre beaucoup de beau Monde, qui y vont prendre l'Air. Il y a de tres belles Maisons, & sur tout Bellsize, où il y a de beaux Jardins & des Courses, &c. pour le Divertissemens de ceux qui y vont boire, &c. Vous pourrez après cela aller voir l'Hotel des Invalides qu'on appelle*

Chelsea-Hospital,

IT is very fine and the Gardens very well kept. You have here also a Statute of K. *Charles* II. who founded this Hospital: And an Inscription, which says that *Charles* II. began it, that *James* II. continued it, and that K. *William* III. and Queen *Mary* finisht it. The Oeconomy observed here is admirable and it is worth any Body's while to see the Poor maimed Soldiers Dine. Thence you go to see the Town of *Chelsea* which is very fine and where the Duke of *Beaufort* and the Bp. of *Winchester* have each a fine House. Then you'll go by Water to

Chelsea-Hospital,

IL est tres beau les *Jardins* en sont tres bien Entretenus & vous y verrez encore une Statuë de Charles II. qui l'a commencé: & une Inscription sur la maison qui marque que Charles II. l'a commencé, que Jaques II. l'a continué, & que Guillaume III. & Marie l'ont achevé. L'Oeconomie y est admirable & merite qu'on y voye diner les pauvres Soldats Estropiez. Dela vous pourrez aller voir le Village de Chelsea, qui est tres beau, & où l'Evêque de Winchester, & le Duc de Beaufort, ont chacun un bel Hotel. Ensuite vous prendrez un bateau & vous ferez mener a

Vaux-Hall,

HEre is a very fine Garden called *Spring-Garden,* which deserves well to be seen, and then returning towards *London* by Land you come to

Vaux-Hall,

OU il y a un tres beau *Jardin,* qu'on appelle Spring-Garden, qui merite bien d'estre Vu, & en revenant vers Londres par terre vous viendrez au

to the Archiepiscopal Palace of *Lambeth* where his Grace the Archbishop of *Canterbury* resides; he keeps open Table there every *Saturday*, and all Men of Letters and Gentlemen are very well received. If you will not go first to *Chelsea* when you go this Tour, you may go by *Hide-Park* Corner to *Kensington*, as soon as you come into *Hide-Park*, you go by an Alley lined with Lanthorns made after the *Dutch* Fashion to the Palace of

au Palais *Archiepiscopal* Lambeth, où *sa Grandeur Monseig. l'Archevêque* de Canterbury *fait sa Residence; il y tient Table ouverte tous les Samedy, & les Gens de Lettres ou les Personnes de Distinction y sont tres bien reçus. Si vous ne voulez pas aller premierement a* Chelsea *en faisant ce Tour vous irez par* Hide-Parc *Corner à* Kensington. *De là vous entrez dans* Hide-Parc, *qui vous mene par une Allée bordées de Lanternes faites à la* Hollandois *au*

Kensington,

Palais de Kensington

THis Palace which King *William* bought from the Earl of *Nottingham*, was inlarged and beautified by that Prince who died there, as well as Queen *Anne*; K. *George* has lately made considerable Additions and magnificent Imbellishments to the same. There are excellent Pictures in this Palace, and the Garden of it is very fine.

CE *Palais que le Roy* Guillaume *achetta du Comte de* Nottingham, *fut agrandi & embelli par ce Prince qui y mourut, aussi bien que la Reine* Anne. *Le Roy George y a depuis peu fait des Additions considerables, & des Embellissemens magnifiques. Il y a d'excellens Tableaux dans ce Palais. Les Jardins en sont tres beaux. De là vous pourrez*

fine. From hence you may go to *Chelsea*, and thence to *Lambeth*. You may go another Day in a Coach or by Water to

rez aller à *Chelsey* & à *Lambeth*. *Vous pourrez un outre Jour prendre un Carosse où un Bateau & aller a*

Richmond,

WHere his Royal Highness the Prince of *Wales* has a fine House. The Green, the fine Country Houses and Seats, the Park, the noble Prospect you have from the Hill of the magnificent Seats on the Banks of the River make this Place the most agreable of any about *London*. From thence you may go to

Richmond,

OU sont Altesse Royale le Prince de Galles, à une belle Maison. Le Prez qu'on appelle le Green, les belles Maisons de Plaisans, le beau Parc, la belle Vuë qu'on y a de dessus la Montagne des magnifiques Maisons qui sont sur les deux bords de la Riviere, font que cet Endroit est l'un des plus agreable qu'il y ait aux environs de Londres. *De là on peut aller a*

Hampton-Court,

WHich is but three Miles from *Richmond*; it is the finest Palace in *England*, the *West* Front was built by Cardinal *Woolsey :* You may easily distinguish what that Cardinal has built, for all the fine House to the East was built by K.
Wil-

Hampton-Court,

QUi n'en est qu'a une Lieuë c'est le plus beau Palais de l'Angleterre ; le Front qui est vers l'Occident a eté bati par le Cardinal Woolsey : *vous pourrez aisèment distinguer ce que ce Cardinal en a bati, car tout le beau Corps de Logis qui est vers l'Orient*

William III. and K. *George* has finish'd the Apartments of it, and laid the Floors and Wainscoted them.   In this Palace are the Cartoons of the famous *Raphael,* and several other admirable Paintings and Hangings. The Gardens, Waterworks, the Park, and every thing belonging to it is extraordinary fine.   There are in this Palace fifteen hundred Rooms besides Closets. The great Stairs is excellently well painted. From thence you may go to

l'Orient a eté bati par le feu Roy Guillaume III, *& le Roy* George *a fait finis les Appartemens, & les boiser & plancher. On y void les* Cartoons *du fameux* Raphael, *& plusieurs autres Pieces & Tapisseries admirables. Les Jardins, les Jetts d'Eaux, les Parcs, & enfin tout ce qui en depend est extraordinairement beau. Il y a dans ce Palais quinze Cent Chambres, outre les Cabinets.   Le grand Escalier est Peint d'un Gout excellent. De la vous pourrez aller à* Windsor *en Anglois,*

Windsor-Castle.

THis Palace was built by K. *Edward* III. is situated on a Hill near the Banks of the *Thames* in the Borough of *Windsor.* Several Kings have made Additions to the same, so that it has two Courts, which divide three great Piles of Buildings. But the outsides of this Castle, nor the Entrance are neither fine nor

Windsor-Castle.

CE *Palais qui a eté bati par* Edouard III. *est situé sur une hauteur près du Bord de la* Thamise, *dans le Bourg de* Windsor. *Plusieurs Rois y ont ajouté des Embellissemens, de sorte qu'il est composé de deux Cours, qui partagent trois grands Corps de Logis. Mais les dehors ni l'Entrée n'en sont ni beaux ni Reguliers. Vous trouvez*

nor regular; as you go into it you come first to the Chapel of St. *George*, where the Knights Companions of the Order of St. *George*, or the Garter, are Installed: At the end of this Chapel is the Seat, Marks of Dignity, and Ensign of the King, Sovereign of this Order. On the Right-hand of this is the Seat of the Prince of *Wales*, on the Left that of the Duke of *York* the King's Brother. On the Right and Left of the said Chapel are those of the twenty four Knights, on each is their Ensign with their Coat of Arms, *&c.* along those Seats you see the Names of all the Knights who have filled it since the Institution of the Order. From hence you will go to see the Apartments, which are very magnificent. King *William* had the Stairs painted, as also the Gallery and some Ceilings. The Gallery is near the Chapel of the Castle; on one side of this Gallery is *John* King of France

vez d'abord la Chapelle de St. George, où se fait l'Installation des Chevaliers de l'Ordre de St. George, où de la Jarretiere: Au bout de cette Chapelle est le Siege, le Marquez d'Honneurs & Etendart du Roy Souverain de l'Ordre. A Droite est celui du Prince de Galles, & a Gauche celui du Duc d'York, Frere du Roy. A Droite & a Gauche de la dite Chapelle, font ceux des Vingtquatre Chevaliers, avec chacun son Etendart avec ses Armes, &c. le long du Siege se voyent les Noms de tous les Chevaliers qui l'ont rempli depuis l'Institution de l'Ordre. De la vous irez voir les Apartemens, qui font tres Magnifiques. Le feu Roy Guillaume en a faite Peindre l'Escalier, la Gallerie, & quelques Platfonds. La Gallerie est proche de la Chapelle du Chateau: Sur un coté de cette Gallerie on void Jean Roy de France, & deux autres Roys qu'on

France and two other Kings led as Prisoners: At the end of this Gallery is King *William* on a Throne painted to the greatest Perfection. The Air is extraordinary good here, and from the Terrass that goes round the Apartments you have one of the finest Prospects in *Europe*. Here is a very fine Park and a Forest, where the Kings often go a Hunting. It is on the great Tower of this Castle that the Heirs of the late Duke of *Marlborough* are to set up a Standard every third Day of *August* for ever, in Memory of the Battle of *Hochstet*, which that Hero won on that Day. And from thence you may go to the

qu'on mene Prisoniers; Au bout de cette Gallerie, le Roy Guillaume est representé sur un Throne, il est Peint dans la derniere Perfection. On y Jouït d'un Air tres pur, & de dessus la Terrasse qui Regne a l'entour des Appartemens, on a une des belles vuës de l'Europe. Il y a un tres beau Parc, & une belle Forest, où le Roy va souvent a la Chasse. C'est sur la grand Tour de ce Chateau que les Heritiers du feu Duc de Marlborough *doivent arborer un etendart tous les troisiemes d'*Aoust *a pepetuité en Memoire de la Battaille d'*Hochstet, *que ce Hero gagna ce jour. Et de là si vous voulez vous pourrez aller à*

University of Oxford.

*Université d'*Oxford

IT is one of the most ancient, most famous and indisputably the largest University in all *Europe* : The magnificence of its Colleges, which are nineteen in num-

C'Est une des plus ancienne, des plus fameuse & sans contredit la plus grande Université de toute l'Europe : La magnificence de ses Colleges, qui sont au nombre de Dixneuf, outre

number, beside seven or or eight Halls, or inferior Colleges; that of its *Publick Buildings*, *viz.* the *Library*, the *Theater*, the *Musæum*, and the stately Colleges of *Christ-Church*, of *Queens*, of *Brazen-Nose*, of *Merton*, of *University*, of *Jesus*, and of *Magdalen*, is extraordinary and surprising. Each College has a Chapel, a Library, and Gardens. In short, the Number, the Quality and Erudition of its Doctors and Students, make it the admiration of all the Strangers who come to see it. The Situation of it is the most wholsome and most agreeable in *Europe*. When you have spent two or three Days to view the Beauties of it you may go see the

outre sept a huit Halles, ou Colleges inferieurs, celle de ses Ediffices Publics, sçavoir, sa Bibliotheque, son Theatre, son Musæum, & des beaux Colleges de Christ-Church, de la Reine, de Brazen-Nose, de Merton, de l' Université, de Jesus, & de la Madeleine, sont extraordinaires & surprise. Chaque College a sa Chapelle, sa Bibliotheque, & ses Jardins. Enfin, le Nombre, la Qualité, & l' Erudition de ses Docteurs & Etudiens, la rendent un sujet d' admiration a tous les Etrangers qui la vont voir. Sa Situation est des plus saines & des plus agreablés de l' Europe. Apres avoir passez deux ou trois Jours à en voir les Beautés vous pourrez aller voir

The *Castle* of Bleinheim.

Le Chateau de *Bleinheim.*

THis is the famous Building which the *English* Nation has erected with all possible Magnificence for the late Prince

C'Est ce fameux Ediffice que la Nation Angloise a fait eriger avec toute la Magnificence possible pour le feu Prince

Prince and Duke of *Marlborough*, in order to perpetuate the Signal Victory which that Hero obtained over the *French* and *Bavarians* at the Villages of *Bleinheim* and *Hochstet*, where the Mareschal *Tallard* was taken Prisoner, and about 40000 Men were killed, drowned, or taken. This Castle is about six Miles distance from *Oxford*, near the Borough of *Woodstock*. The Architecture thereof is one of the most regular, the Building is very large, the Bridge before it, its Park, Allies, Furniture, and Paintings, and indeed all that is there is fine and very magnificent, and shews the generous Spirit, the Acknowledgement and Wealth of this Nation. From hence you may go to see

Prince & Duc de Marlborough, afin de perpetuer la Victorie signalée que ce Hero remporta sur les François & Bavarois aux Villages de Bleinheim & Hochstet, où le Mareschal de Tallard fut fait Prisonier, & environ 40000 Hommes tués, noyez, où pris. Ce Chateau est a environ six Milles d' Oxford, pres du Bourg de Woodstock. L' Architecture en est des plus reguliere, l' Ediffice est tres vaste, le Pont qui est devant, son Parc, ses Allées, ses Meubles, & Tableaux ; enfin tout en est beau & tres magnifiques, & fait voir le genereux Esprit la Reconnoissance & l' Opulence de cette Nation. De là vous pourrez aller voir

The University of Cambridge.

L' Université de Cambridge.

THo' this University is neither so ancient

QUoique cette Université ne soit ni si ancienne,

ent nor so large as that of *Oxford*, it is however very fine ; it has fine Colleges, especially *Kings-College*, the Chapel of which is one of the finest in *Europe* : Its Air is not so wholsome as that of *Oxford*; but its Colleges are endowed with very large Revenues; and we may affirm, that it might be reckon'd one of the finest in *Europe*, if *Oxford* did not exceed it in number of Colleges and Students. These two Universities are within fifty Miles from *London*, and about fifty Miles from each other. After you have seen them, and returned to *London*, you may go by Water to see the fine

ni si grand que celle de Oxford, *elle ne laissé pas d'etre tres belle*; *elle a de tres beaux Colleges entre autre* Kings-College, *dont la Chapelle est une des plus belles de l'*Europe. *Elle ne joüit pas d'un Air aussi sain que celle d'* Oxford, *mais ses Colleges sont douez de tres bons Revenus, & on peut dire qu'elle passeroit pour une des plus belles de l'* Europe, *si* Oxford *ne la surpassoit en nombre de Colleges & d'Etudians. Ces deux Universités sont à cinquante Milles de* Londres, *& a cinquante Milles l'une de l'autre. Apres que vous les aurez vuës & que vous serez de retour à* Londres *il ne faut pas manquer de prendre un Bateau & d'aller par eau a*

Hospital of Greenwich.

L' Hopital de *Greenwich.*

AS you go down the River you will be surpris'd at the vast number of Ships that line both sides of the River, and look like a Forest for about

EN descendant la Rivierre vous serez surpris de la grand quantité de Vaisseaux qui bordent les deux cotés de la Rivierre pendant près d'une

 lieuë

bout three Miles. When you have paſſed a new Church, which is on your Left, you come to *Deptford*, where a new Royal Storehouſe for Proviſions and Naval Stores for Shipping was lately built; and then you come to *Greenwich*: You will go immediately to ſee the magnificent Hoſpital which King *William* III. has built here for Invalid Seamen; it is a Structure anſwerable to the Magnificence of the King of a Nation which is the Queen of the Seas. The ſecond Wing, which is to be equal to that which is now finiſh'd, goes but ſlowly forwards; but in the other the Lodgings, Courts, Halls, are very fine and magnificent. You muſt not omit to ſee the fine Hall, in the Ceiling of which King *William* III. and Queen *Mary* his Spouſe are painted with the Deities in their proper Symbols; and all the Stores and Tackles of Ships admirably well drawn. From thence

lieuë & qui reſſemblent a une Foreſt. Apres que vous aurez paſſez une Egliſe neuve qui eſt a votre Gauche, vous viendrez a Deptford, *où l'on a depuis peu bati un beau Magazin Royal, pour les Proviſions & Agrets des Vaiſſeaux; & enſuite vous viendrez a* Greenwich : *Vous y irez d' abord voir le magnifique Hopital que le Roy* Guillaume III. *y a fait batir pour les Matelots Invalides; c'eſt un Edifice digne de la Magnificence du Roy d'une Nation qui eſt la Reine des Mers. La ſeconde Aile qui ſera egale à celle qui eſt finie, ne s'avance que fort lentement; les Logemens, les Cours, les Sales, en ſont tres belles & magnifiques. Il ne faut pas oublier de voir la belle Sale, dans le Platfond de laquelle on void le Roy* Guillaume *& la Reine* Marie *ſon Eſpouſe, avec les Divinités dans leurs Symboles; & tous les Agrets & Attiraile de Vaiſſeaux admirablement bien repreſentes. De la vous irez voir le*

thence you may go to the Park, the King's-House, and the Royal Observatory. Afterwards you may go on the Hill called *Black-Heath,* where are very fine Buildings, and whence you will have a moft charming View of *London,* the River, and all the Country around.

These are all the Places we thought worthy of your Curiofity, there are undoubtedly many others that deferve your Notice, efpecially the great Foundery at *Woolwich,* within two Miles of *Greenwich;* and where you will be furpriz'd at the vaft quantity of Canon, *&c.* that are there; but this Volume is too large already, therefore I will now only fet down here the Prices of Hackney - Coaches, Stage-Coaches, and Boats, that you may not be impofed upon.

Coachmen and Watermen are (in all Places) for the moft part, rude Fellows, that will hearken

le Parc, la Maifon Royale, & l' Obfervatoire Royal. Enfuite vous irez fur la Montagne qu'on appelle Black-Heath, où il y a des Batimens fuperbes, & d' où vous aurez une vuë de Londres, de la Riviere, & du Païfage d' alentour, qui eft tout a fait charmante.

Voila tout ce que l'on a jugé de lieux digne de votre Curiofité; il y en a fans contredit plufieurs autres que meriteroit votre attention, fur tout la grande Fonderie de Woolwich, qui eft a deux Milles par de la Greenwich, & dont vous aurez lieu d'être furpris par la quantité de Canons, &c. qui y font; mais ce Volume n'eft deja que trop etendu. C'eft pourquoi je me borneray a vous marquer les prix des Fiacres, Cochis, & Bateaux, afin qu'on ne vous en impofe point.

Les Cochers & Bateliers, font (en tous lieux) pour la pluspart des bruteaux, qui n'entendent aucune Raifon;

ken

ken to no Reason; therefore if they happen to fall out with you, or ask you more than the Prices following, you must give them what they ask and complain to the Commissioners, who will force the Coachmen to do you Justice; and to Watermens-Hall, who will do the same with the Watermen. In order to this, if you are aggriev'd, you must take the Number of the Coach, which is on the Door of the Coach; or that of the Boat, which is commonly above the Thofts and near the Oar, and giving the said Number, the Coachman or Waterman will be forc'd to answer your Complaints. The Commissioners for Hackney-Coaches meet in *Surrey-street* in the *Strand*, and the Waterman's-Hall is on the *Thames* near *London*-Bridge.

son ; de forte que s'ils difputent avec vous, & vous demandent plus que les Prix fuivants ; il le leur faut payer, & s'en plaindre aux Commiffaires, qui vous feront Juftice des Cochers ; & a la Halle des Bateliers, où on vous la fera des Bateliers. Pour cet effet fi vous etes grevé, vous prendrés le Numero, qui eft à la Portiere du Fiacre, où en dedans du Bateau un peu au deffous du Bord, par la vous decouvriré l'Agreffeur. Les Commiffaires s'affemblent a Surrey-ftreet *a la* Strand, *& la Halle des Bateliers eft fur le bord de la* Thamife, *proche du Pont de* Londres.

The Rates of Stage-Coaches, Hackney-Coaches, and Watermen.

Les Prix des Coches, des Fiacres, & des Bateaux.

Coachmens Rates.

Les Prix de Cochils.

	s.	d.		s.	d.
If you take a Coach for a whole Day of 12 Hours you must pay	10	0	Si vous prennez un Fiacre pour un Jour entier de 12 Heures vous en payerez	10	0
If by the Hour you pay for the first Hour	1	6	Si c'est par Heure vous payerez, pour la premiere Heure	1	6
And for every Hour after the first	1	0	Et pour chaque Heure apres la premiere	1	0
For every distance not exceeding a Mile and an half	1	0	Pour chaque distance n'excedant point une demi lieuë	1	0
For such as do not exceed two Miles	1	6	Pour celles qui n'excedent point deux Milles	1	6
From Westminster-Hall to St. Paul's	1	6	Depuis la Salle de Westminster jusqu'à St. Paul	1	6
From St. Paul's to Southwark beyond the Bridge	1	6	Depuis St. Paul jusqu'à Southwark dela Pont	1	6
From the Royal-Exchange to Somerset-House	1	0	Depuis la Bourse-Royale jusqu'au Hotel de Somerset	1	0

From

De

From the Royal-Exchange to Charing-Cross } 1 6

From the Royal-Exchange to St. James's } 2 0

From the Royal-Exchange to the two Playhouses } s. d. } 1 6

From St. James's to Kensington } 2 0

From Charing-Cross to the Tower or Custom-House } 2 6

And so from all other Places proportionable to the Distance, at One Shilling *per* Mile.

For the Stage-Coach from London to Hampton-Court } 2 6

From London to Windsor } 3 6

From London to Oxford } 10 0

From London to Cambridge } 10 0

Depuis la Bourse Royale jusqu'au Cheval Bronze } 1 6

Depuis la Bourse Royale jusqu'au St. James } 2 0

Depuis la ditte Bourse jusqu'aux deux Commedies } s. d. } 1 6

Depuis St. James, jusqu'à Kensing-ton. } 2 0

Depuis le Cheval de Bronze jusqu'à la Tour ou Douane } 2 6

Et ainsi de tous autres endroits selon la Distance des Lieux à proportion d'un Chelin par Mille.

Pour le Cache de Londres à Hampton Court } 2 6

Ditto de Londres à Windsor } 3 6

Ditto de Londres à Oxford } 10 0

Ditto de Londres à Cambridge } 10 0

Watermens Rates.			*Les Prix des Bateaux.*	
to an Oar.			**a la Oar.**	
From *Whitehall* to *London-Bridge*	0	6	De *Whitehal au* Pont *de* Londres	6 *Sous*
From the Bridge to *Lambeth* or *Vaux-Hall*	1	6	*De puis le Pont* à Lambeth *ou* Vaux-Hall	1 *Cheling*
From *Whiteball* to *Lambeth* or *Vaux-Hall*	0	8	*Depuis* Whitehal à Lambeth *ou* Vaux-Hall	8 *Sous*
To cross the River	0	4	*Pour traverser la* Rivierre	4 *Sous*
to a Sculler.			**a la Sculler.**	
From *Whitehall* to *London-Bridge*	0	3	De Whitehall *au* Pont *de* Londres	3 *Sous*
From the Bridge to *Lambeth,* or *Vaux-Hall*	0	6	*De puis le Pont* à Lambeth, *ou* Vaux-Hall	6 *Sous*
From *Whiteball* to *Lambeth,* or *Vaux-Hall*	0	4	*Depuis* Whitehal à Lambeth, *ou* Vaux-Hall	4 *Sous*
To cross the River	0	2	*Pour traverser la* Rivierre	2 *Sous*

F I N I S.

BIBLIOTHÈQUE DE L'ARSENAL

and thus

www.ingramcontent.com/pod-product-compliance
Ingram Content Group UK Ltd.
Pitfield, Milton Keynes, MK11 3LW, UK
UKHW022241120726
13694UKWH00003B/919